Richard F. Clarke

The ministry of Jesus

Meditations for six months

Richard F. Clarke

The ministry of Jesus
Meditations for six months

ISBN/EAN: 9783744646741

Printed in Europe, USA, Canada, Australia, Japan

Cover: Foto ©Lupo / pixelio.de

More available books at **www.hansebooks.com**

The Ministry of Jesus.

MEDITATIONS FOR SIX MONTHS.

BY RICHARD F. CLARKE, S.J.

LONDON
CATHOLIC TRUTH SOCIETY,
18, WEST SQUARE, S.E.

1892.

PREFACE.

In this little volume I have proposed for meditation the chief miracles, parables, and other incidents and discourses in the Public Life of our Lord. At the head of each meditation I have indicated the passage from the Gospels on which it is based. But lest some should find it inconvenient to refer to it, I have given in each case a short summary of the passage.

In the order of events I have followed Father Coleridge's *Vita Vitæ Nostræ*, and in matters of interpretation I have for the most part kept close to Maldonatus' Commentary on the Gospels.

These Meditations are calculated to fill up just half the year. Any one commencing them after the octave of Corpus Christi will find that they will carry him on to the beginning of Advent or thereabouts.

I have not attempted to give any rules respecting preparatory prayer, or good resolutions at the end, but I would remind the reader that if nothing can prosper without the help of God, least of all can meditations be made successfully unless His grace be given, and that the test of a good meditation is not mere pious thoughts or affections, but the practice during the day of the virtues pondered over in the morning meditation.

CONTENTS.

	page
FIRST WEEK:	
Sunday.—The Baptism of Jesus	1
Monday.—His Fasting	2
Tuesday.—His Temptation	3
Wednesday.—The Lamb of God	4
Thursday.—The First Disciples	5
Friday.—Nathanael	6
Saturday.—The Marriage at Cana	7
SECOND WEEK:	
Sunday.—The Expulsion of the Traders from the Temple	8
Monday.—The Test of Jesus' Mission	9
Tuesday.—The Visit of Nicodemus	10
Wednesday.—The New Birth	11
Thursday.—The Heavenly Gift	12
Friday.—The Brazen Serpent	13
Saturday.—St. John the Baptist's Testimony to Jesus	14
THIRD WEEK:	
Sunday.—The Well of Samaria	15
Monday.—The Living Water	16
Tuesday.—The True and False Worship	17
Wednesday.—The Conversion of the Samaritans	18
Thursday.—The Ripening Harvest	19
Friday.—The Healing of the Nobleman's Son	20
Saturday.—The Synagogue at Nazareth	21
FOURTH WEEK:	
Sunday.—A Prophet in His own Country	22
Monday.—The Anger of the Nazarenes	23
Tuesday.—The Call of the Fishermen	24
Wednesday.—The Synagogue at Capharnaum	25
Thursday.—The Casting Out of the Devil	26
Friday.—The Healing of Peter's Wife's Mother	27
Saturday.—The Work of Jesus at Capharnaum	28

FIFTH WEEK:

Sunday.—First Beatitude: Blessed are the Poor in Spirit 29
Monday.—Second Beatitude: Blessed are the Meek 30
Tuesday.—Third Beatitude: Blessed are they that mourn 31
Wednesday.—Fourth Beatitude: Blessed are they that hunger and thirst after Justice 32
Thursday.—Fifth Beatitude: Blessed are the Merciful 33
Friday.—Sixth Beatitude: Blessed are the Clean of Heart 34
Saturday.—Seventh Beatitude: Blessed are the Peacemakers 35

SIXTH WEEK:

Sunday.—Eighth Beatitude: Blessed are they that suffer Persecution for Justice' sake 36
Monday.—Christians the Salt and the Light of the World 37
Tuesday.—The Fulfilling of the Law 38
Wednesday.—On Alms and Prayers in Public 39
Thursday.—On the Laying up of Treasure .. 40
Friday.—On Purity of Intention 41
Saturday.—On Confidence in God 42

SEVENTH WEEK:

Sunday.—On Rash Judgment 43
Monday.—On the Efficacy of Prayer 44
Tuesday.—On Judging by Results 45
Wednesday.—The House upon the Rock .. 46
Thursday.—The Miraculous Draught of Fishes 47
Friday.—The Healing of the Leper 48
Saturday.—The Healing of the Paralytic .. 49

EIGHTH WEEK:

Sunday.—The Vocation of St. Matthew .. 50
Monday.—The Feast in Matthew's House .. 51
Tuesday.—The Miracle at the Probatic Pool .. 52
Wednesday.—Our Lord retires before His Enemies 53
Thursday.—The Corn-plucking on the Sabbath 54

	page
Friday.—The Jews rebuked	55
Saturday.—The Spirit and the Letter	56

NINTH WEEK:

	page
Sunday.—The Enrolment of the Apostles	57
Monday.—The Sermon on the Plain	58
Tuesday.—The Centurion's Servant	59
Wednesday.—The Widow of Naim	60
Thursday.—The Visit of St. John's Disciples	61
Friday.—Our Lord's witness to St. John the Baptist	62
Saturday.—The Result of neglected Graces	63

TENTH WEEK:

	page
Sunday.—The Divine Consoler	64
Monday.—The Conversion of St. Mary Magdalen	65
Tuesday.—The Blasphemy of the Pharisees	66
Wednesday.—The Sin against the Holy Ghost	67
Thursday.—Idle Words	68
Friday.—True Relationship to Christ	69
Saturday.—The Sower and the Seed	70

ELEVENTH WEEK:

	page
Sunday.—The Roadside and Stony Ground	71
Monday.—The Thorny Ground	72
Tuesday.—The Good Ground	73
Wednesday.—The Parable of the Cockle	74
Thursday.—The Seed cast into the Ground	75
Friday.—The Parable of the Mustard-seed	76
Saturday.—The Treasure hid in the Field	77

TWELFTH WEEK:

	page
Sunday.—The Pearl of Great Price	78
Monday.—The Parable of the Leaven	79
Tuesday.—The Stilling of the Tempest	80
Wednesday.—The Legion of Devils cast out	81
Thursday.—The Old and the New	82
Friday.—The Healing of the Woman with an Issue of Blood	83
Saturday.—The Raising of the Daughter of Jairus	84

THIRTEENTH WEEK:

	page
Sunday.—The sending out of the Apostles to preach	85

Monday.—The Instructions for the Journey .. 86
Tuesday.—Our Lord's care of His Servants .. 87
Wednesday.—The Warfare of the Gospel .. 88
Thursday.—The Recompense of Charity .. 89
Friday.—The Death of St. John the Baptist .. 90
Saturday.—The Return of the Apostles .. 91
FOURTEENTH WEEK:
Sunday.—The Feeding of the Five Thousand .. 92
Monday.—The Gathering up of the Fragments 93
Tuesday.—Jesus appears walking upon the Lake 94
Wednesday.—St. Peter walks upon the Water .. 95
Thursday.—The Meat that perisheth 96
Friday.—The Bread from Heaven 97
Saturday.—The Saving Will of God 98
FIFTEENTH WEEK:
Sunday.—The Murmuring of the Jews 99
Monday.—The Question of Unbelief 100
Tuesday.—Backsliding Disciples 101
Wednesday.—The Unwashed Hands 102
Thursday.—The Growth of Corrupt Traditions 103
Friday.—Evil Thoughts 104
Saturday.—The Sinfulness of Evil Thoughts .. 105
SIXTEENTH WEEK:
Sunday.—The Syrophœnician Woman 106
Monday.—The Deaf and Dumb Man healed .. 107
Tuesday —The Sign from Heaven 108
Wednesday.—The Leaven of the Pharisees .. 109
Thursday.—The Blind Man at Bethsaida .. 110
Friday.—The Confession of St. Peter 111
Saturday.—The Promise to St. Peter 112
SEVENTEENTH WEEK:
Sunday.—The Approaching Passion 113
Monday.—The Doctrine of the Cross 114
Tuesday.—Loss and Gain 115
Wednesday.—The Transfiguration 116
Thursday.—The Healing of the Boy who was possessed 117
Friday.—The Tribute-money 118
Saturday.—The Dispute among the Apostles .. 119

EIGHTEENTH WEEK:
  Sunday.—On Scandal 120
  Monday.—On Fraternal Charity 121
  Tuesday.—The Sacrament of Matrimony .. 122
  Wednesday.—The Feast of Tabernacles .. 123
  Thursday.—Our Lord in the Temple 124
  Friday.—The Woman taken in Adultery .. 125
  Saturday.—The Man born Blind 126
NINETEENTH WEEK:
  Sunday.—The Good Shepherd 127
  Monday.—The Spirit of the Gospel 128
  Tuesday.—Some Conditions of following Christ 129
  Wednesday.—The Mission of the Seventy .. 130
  Thursday.—The Good Samaritan 131
  Friday.—Martha and Mary 132
  Saturday.—How to Pray 133
TWENTIETH WEEK:
  Sunday.—The Divided House 134
  Monday.—The Divine Maternity 135
  Tuesday.—The Rich Fool 136
  Wednesday.—Watch! 137
  Thursday.—The Unfruitful Fig-tree 138
  Friday.—The Narrow Gate 139
  Saturday.—On Self-Exaltation 140
TWENTY-FIRST WEEK:
  Sunday.—The Great Supper 141
  Monday.—The Lost Sheep 142
  Tuesday.—The Lost Groat 143
  Wednesday.—The Prodigal Son: his Departure 144
  Thursday.—   „   his Repentance 145
  Friday.—   „   his Return .. 146
  Saturday.—The Unjust Steward 147
TWENTY-SECOND WEEK:
  Sunday.—On the Use of Riches 148
  Monday.—The Rich Glutton 149
  Tuesday.—The Raising of Lazarus 150
  Wednesday.—The Assembly of the Pharisees .. 151
  Thursday.—The Ten Lepers 152
  Friday.—The Unjust Judge 153
  Saturday.—The Pharisee and the Publican .. 154

TWENTY-THIRD WEEK:
Sunday.—The Necessity of Humility 155
Monday.—The Rich Young Man 156
Tuesday.—The Evangelical Counsels 157
Wednesday.—The Signs of His Approach .. 158
Thursday.—The Suddenness of His Coming .. 159
Friday.—Coming Troubles 160
Saturday.—The Labourers in the Vineyard .. 161
TWENTY-FOURTH WEEK:
Sunday.—The Petition of the Sons of Zebedee.. 162
Monday.—The Blind Men of Jericho 163
Tuesday.—The Conversion of Zaccheus .. 164
Wednesday.—The Lord and his Servants .. 165
Thursday.—The Procession of Palms 166
Friday.—Christ weeps over Jerusalem 167
Saturday.—On Death to the World 168
TWENTY-FIFTH WEEK:
Sunday.—The Barren Fig-tree 169
Monday.—On Confidence in Prayer 170
Tuesday.—Our Lord's Authority to Teach .. 171
Wednesday.—The Disobedient Sons 172
Thursday.—The Question of the Sadducees .. 173
Friday.—The Vineyard and the Husbandmen .. 174
Saturday.—The Wedding of the King's Son .. 175
TWENTY-SIXTH WEEK:
Sunday.—Cæsar and God 176
Monday.—The Widow's Mite 177
Tuesday.—The Great Commandment 178
Wednesday.—" Woe to you, Scribes and Pharisees " 179
Thursday.—The Parable of the Ten Virgins .. 180
Friday.—The Parable of the Talents 181
Saturday.—The Final Judgment 182

First Week: Sunday.
The Baptism of Jesus.
St. Matt. iii. 13—17.

Our Lord bids farewell to His holy Mother; makes His way to the Jordan; is baptized by St. John amid a crowd of sinners, and is proclaimed by the Voice from Heaven the Beloved Son of God.

1. For thirty years Jesus had dwelt in sweet companionship with His holy Mother. Never since the world began had there been any intercourse so full of unspeakable delight as that of Jesus and Mary. Now the time had come to break the bond: it was like the tearing asunder of their loving hearts for them to part. Yet Christ goes on His way with the greatest cheerfulness and joy: for it was the will of God that He should forsake His Mother, and the motto of His life was: "Lo, I come to do Thy will, O My God."

2. It is the same Divine guidance that leads Him to the Jordan, to be baptized among sinners, just as if He, the Lamb of God, were Himself a sinner. Yet He never hesitates for an instant. It was the will of God, and therefore it is His greatest joy to do what men would esteem so misleading and ill-judged, so fatal to the success of His future Mission. Do I thus implicitly obey the will of God?

3. Obedience and humility are the surest way of winning honour from God. He loves to exalt the humble, to pour Divine gifts upon the obedient. A Voice from Heaven declares Him Who had thus humbled Himself to be the well-beloved Son of God. The Holy Spirit descending in visible form proclaims wisdom to be the special privilege of the obedient.

First Week: Monday.
His Fasting.

St. Matt. iv. 1.

After His Baptism, our Lord was driven by the Spirit into the desert to be tempted by the devil. Previously to the temptation He had fasted for forty days and forty nights, and dwelt among wild beasts.

1. It was under the impulse of the Holy Spirit that our Lord went out into the desert to be tempted. Men often think that when temptations assail them it is their own fault or a punishment for their sins, and lose courage accordingly. They forget that may be the Holy Spirit is guiding them in the same path in which He guided the Son of God: that they are but following in His sacred footsteps. Temptation is not only permitted by God, but He ordains it for the greater sanctification of His elect.

2. Our Lord prepared for His temptation by a long fast. Did He need it as a means of overcoming the rebellion of nature? How could He, the spotless Lamb of God, whose Human Nature was joined in closest union to the Divinity, need any aid to repel the assaults of Satan? No, it was for my sake. It was that I might have strength to overcome, it was to earn graces for me that I see Him pale and faint and wan after His long and painful fast.

3. He was with the wild beasts, in solitudes far removed from all human intercourse, among animals wild and savage, who were, however, obedient unto Him as their Master and King. Christ as Man was Lord of all creation. It was sin that made the brutes our enemies. No creature on earth can really harm us except by reason of sin. To those who love God all things work together for good.

First Week: Tuesday.
His Temptation.
St. Matt. iv. 2—11.

At the end of forty days Satan comes to Jesus, disguised, it is said, as one of the hermits who lived in the neighbourhood of the Jordan, and pours into His ears his infernal suggestions of sin.

1. How utterly repulsive to the Son of God must have been the presence of the evil one. He Who had been nursed in Mary's bosom, and carried in the faithful arms of His dear foster-father St. Joseph, now allowed Himself to be borne hither and thither by the being whom He loathed and hated with His whole soul. This was indeed a painful beginning of His Sacred Ministry.

2. Why did Christ allow Himself to be tempted? Did He not already know perfectly every wile and deceit of Satan? Yes, He knew them, but not by experience. He wanted us to have the consolation of knowing that He suffered being tempted; that He endured the misery of being haunted with the foul suggestions of Hell: and that therefore He, the sinless Lamb of God, knows how to succour those who are assailed by Satan's evil suggestions. With what confidence, then, can I appeal to Him to aid me when I am tempted!

3. Observe our Lord's manner of dealing with the tempter. There is no arguing with him, no discussion. Our Lord deals with the enemy promptly, boldly, firmly, with decision. Sharp and clear is His answer, and very unmistakeable is the rebuff given to His assailant. When Christ says, "Get thee hence,' Satan is glad to leave Him. So we should meet temptation, promptly, boldly, fearlessly, and then Satan will be glad to leave us.

First Week: Wednesday.
The Lamb of God.
St. John i. 29—34.

St. John the Baptist, seeing our Lord approaching, cries aloud : "Behold the Lamb of God, behold Him Who taketh away the sins of the world."

1. The name by which St. John first greeted Jesus was that of the Lamb of God. All names given in Scripture by Divine inspiration are exactly descriptive of those on whom they are conferred. Hence we learn that the prominent feature in our Lord's character is the gentleness, meekness, simplicity, guilelessness of the lamb. This is what made Him so attractive. His sweetness drew all to Him. He is just the same now. In Heaven He is still the Lamb; still gentle and loving as ever. With what confidence, then, I ought to approach Him and tell Him all my troubles.

2. He is not only the Lamb, but the Lamb *of God*. That winning gentleness and sweetness of His is not merely natural. It is the Divine charity manifesting itself in the Son of God. This must be the sweetness and gentleness at which we must aim. God will give it to all of us if we persevere in seeking it. Even though by nature harsh, God can make us gentle and meek.

3. What was the office of the Lamb of God, the work He was sent to do? St. John tells us that it was to take away the sins of the world. Meekness has a wonderful power—"the meek shall possess the land." Meekness takes away sin. To bear reproaches meekly is one of the best means of expiating our own sins and the sins of others, and obtaining for sinners the grace of repentance. Meekness obtains peace for our souls. Alas! how little there is in me of the meekness and gentleness of the Lamb of God!

First Week: Thursday.
The First Disciples.
St. John i. 35—42.

St. Andrew and another of St. John's disciples, hearing their master's words respecting Jesus, follow Him. Andrew afterwards brings his brother Simon to Him, saying: "We have found the Messias."

1. St. John, the first preacher of the Gospel, is a model to all preachers. (*a*) He preaches Jesus. Jesus is the centre of his doctrine. His one object is to turn the hearts of his hearers to Jesus. (*b*) He preaches Jesus under the sweetest and most attractive aspect of "the Lamb of God." He sought to make Jesus the object of their love by dwelling on His gentleness and kindness. (*c*) He does not think of himself. He is only too glad that all his disciples should leave him to follow Jesus. So St. Paul: "We preach not ourselves but Christ Jesus our Lord." Do I in my words and actions forget self and think of Jesus?

2. This kind of teaching soon bears fruit. First one, then another, of his disciples follows the Lamb of God. Our words are sure to bear fruit if they are filled with the love of Jesus. St. John had the happiness of seeing the fruit of his labours; and so in this world or in the world to come will all who point to Jesus, preach Jesus, make Jesus loveable in the eyes of men.

3. One conversion brings another. St. Andrew brings to the fold of Christ his brother Simon, the future Pope, the Rock on which the Church of Christ was to be built. Thus it is with all who obey the voice of their conscience. They are sure to convert others, and insensibly to influence them for good. What happiness for us if we bring only one soul to Jesus!

First Week : Friday.
Nathanael.

St. John i. 45—51.

Philip brings Nathanael to Jesus, Who greets him as "an Israelite indeed, in whom there is no guile." Our Lord tells him that He saw him when Philip found him under the fig-tree; and Nathanael recognizes in Jesus, the Son of God, the King of Israel.

1. Philip is not satisfied with one convert. He seeks another man of good-will, to whom he communicates the joyful tidings that he has found the Messias. Philip was a worthy disciple of his Master. He could not refrain from speaking of Him, and inviting others to enrol themselves under His banner. It is a great mark of love to Jesus, if we are zealous in proclaiming His love to others.

2. Nathanael is incredulous at first; he will not believe that a great Prophet can come from a place of such indifferent repute as Nazareth, but at Philip's suggestion he consents to come and see. Hence learn: (1) Not to be too credulous, but to test and try any reported wonders. (2) Not to be prejudiced against others by reason of their origin. (3) To be willing to inquire into the claims of any who may possibly have a Divine mission to act with Divine authority.

3. Nathanael does not remain long incredulous in the presence of the Son of God. All men of good-will when brought face to face with Truth and with the Catholic Church are irresistibly drawn to it, and need but little evidence to convince them of its Divine character. This recognition of the supernatural is a gift that men possess in proportion to their obedince to the voice of conscience,

First Week: Saturday.
The Marriage at Cana.
St. John ii. 1—11.

At a marriage-feast at Cana, at which our Lord, His holy Mother, and His disciples were present, the wine runs short and our Lady calls the attention of Jesus to the want. At first He seems to rebuke her, but at her bidding He turns six jars of water into the choicest wine. She notices their perplexity and hastens to relieve it.

1. Observe our Lady's thoughtful charity, and her distress at the distress of the entertainers. Her sympathy is not only with what men consider great troubles. Every little inconvenience and annoyance that befalls the friends of Jesus Christ touches her immaculate heart. Learn hence to extend your sympathy to every form of trouble that others suffer.

2. Our Lord at first receives the request of His holy Mother with apparent refusal He pretends that He is not going to grant it. But He is only pretending. So, too, He sometimes pretends to be deaf to the prayers of His faithful servants. They ask, and ask apparently in vain. But it is only that He may be more generous in the end and may reward their perseverance with graces and gifts that they would not have earned had they been heard at first.

3. The wine that our Lord creates is so delicious and superior to what they had had before that the bridegroom is astonished. He need not have wondered. Christ keeps His best gifts to the last. At first trouble, suffering, anxiety; at last peace, joy, happiness, delight. All this, too, even here, to those who are very faithful to God's grace, and how much more in Heaven !

Second Week: Sunday.
The Expulsion of the Traders from the Temple.
St. John ii. 13—17.

Jesus finding in the Temple sellers of oxen, sheep, and doves, and money-changers trading, drives them out with a scourge of small cords, saying to them: "Make not the house of My Father a house of traffic."

1. The anger of the Son of God is roused by the indignity done to His Father's house by those who traded therein. God is always jealous of any encroachment of worldly things on what is consecrated to Him. Woe to those who turn to secular purposes things sacred! How careful we should be to perform all that we have promised to God and to pay Him all that we have offered to Him. Have I ever failed in this respect, or robbed God of what is His due or what I have devoted to be His?

2. There is one respect in which all have failed in giving to God His due. In our prayers, at Holy Mass, in time of meditation, we profess to give our thoughts to God. He therefore has a claim on an exclusive possession of them. Yet how often have I deliberately allowed worldly interests, pleasures, amusements, cares, to occupy His place, and to run riot in my heart even before the altar, so that I have made the house of God a den of thieves!

3. It seems strange that these traders should not have resisted Him Who drove them out. They knew He was right and they were wrong. Nothing is so cowardly as a guilty conscience. A man who knows that he is condemned by the law of God cannot withstand the rebuke of his fellow-men —how much less the Divine anger of the Son of God!

Second Week: Monday.
The Test of Jesus' Mission.

John ii. 18—25.

When the Jews asked Jesus what sign He gave to them that He was acting with God's authority, He answered: "Destroy this temple, and in three days I will raise it up." The Jews thought He meant the Temple of Jerusalem, but He referred to the temple of His Body.

1. There were doubtless some who asked in good faith why Christ took upon Himself the work of reforming the abuse which had crept into the Temple, but others who asked in a spirit of hatred and ill-will. See our Lord's wisdom. His answer is one which would set the former thinking, but only perplex the latter, and render their ill-will greater. This is always God's way. He proposes mysteries for the acceptance of all; men of goodwill ponder on them and are drawn to God; men of ill-will reject the mystery and its Author.

2. Our Lord made the Resurrection the test and corner-stone of His Mission. So the Apostles preached Jesus and the Resurrection. So St. Paul says: "If Christ is not risen, our faith is vain." It is the test of a Christian: Do you believe that Jesus rose again? Thank God for your firm belief in this glorious mystery, and cry out, Lord, I believe!

3. Christ speaks of His Body as the temple of God consecrated to His service. So, too, our bodies are the temples of God. How sacred they ought to be in our eyes! How carefully we should guard them against any defilement of intemperance or impurity, even against a dangerous look, an immodest word, or an unbecoming gesture.

Second Week: Tuesday.
The Visit of Nicodemus.
St. John iii. 1, 2.

Nicodemus, a Pharisee, and a leading man among the Jews, comes by night to declare to our Lord his belief in His Mission and to converse with Him.

1. The Pharisees were the most hopeless class among the Jews: bigoted, proud, selfish, hypocrites. Yet among the Pharisees there was at least one man of good-will who was drawn to our Lord by the words He spoke and the miracles He wrought. Hence learn never to condemn any one because he belongs to a class of evil men. In Sodom was the just Lot; among sinners of abandoned life, St. Mary Magdalen; among the Pharisees, Nicodemus.

2. Nicodemus was a man of loyal soul, but he was timid in his loyalty. He did not dare to face the obloquy which he would have incurred by a public visit to our Lord. Men in high position, and especially men in a false position like that of the Pharisees, are indeed to be pitied. They are often very slaves to the opinion of others and their own supposed reputation or interest. Thank God if you are in a humble position, able to follow your conscience unhindered.

3. Our Lord does not refuse Nicodemus because he was ashamed to come to Him by day, or reproach him with cowardice. He knows the difficulties of his position and makes all allowance for them. He accepts the least mark of good-will, the least approach of the soul to Him. How good He is to us! How considerate to our weakness! How ready to overlook our many slights and our unkindness! This it is that almost compels us to love Him.

Second Week: Wednesday.
The New Birth.
St. John iii. 3—8.

Our Lord declares to Nicodemus the necessity of being born again if we are to see the Kingdom of God, and explains the meaning of this new birth.

1. When Nicodemus declares his belief that Jesus is a teacher sent from God, our Lord answers by what seems beside the mark. He tells him that, "Unless a man be born again, he cannot see the Kingdom of God." His meaning is: "In order to appreciate with Divine faith Who I am, and what means My being sent from God, a man must be born again." It is only the soul that is raised to the supernatural order that can see the Kingdom of God, and recognize who it is that is its King.

2. In the answer of Nicodemus we see the carnal mind still strong within him. He takes a carnal view of the new birth: "How can a man be born when he is old?" So we find that the mysteries of the Kingdom of God are a riddle to all who are not taught of God. They assert that the prophecies of the Old Testament do not primarily refer to our Lord, and explain away even the miracles of the Gospel. The Blessed Eucharist seems to them absurd, and modern miracles a fiction. Thank God for the gift of faith.

3. Our Lord explains to Nicodemus that the spiritual new birth is effected by the secret grace of the Holy Spirit accepted by the soul. It comes noiselessly and like a gentle wind. It is given to all who ask it, and though they know not whence it comes, yet they recognize it as a voice from God. To this Voice, O Jesus, may I be ever obedient!

Second Week: Thursday.
The Heavenly Gift.
St. John iii. 9—13.

Nicodemus asks our Lord how these things of which He speaks are to be done. Jesus tells him that he, as a teacher in Israel, ought to understand them.

1. The surprise that our Lord expresses at Nicodemus' ignorance is meant to teach us that if we are in any position of authority, God expects of us a higher standard of knowledge and practice than He expects of others. There is scarcely any one who is not invested with some authority from God over children, servants, pupils, younger members of our little circle. Some of us have more important and responsible authority. Do we appreciate the account we shall have to give of the use we have made of our authority?

2. Jesus had explained to Nicodemus, by a metaphor from sensible things, the meaning of the new birth which the Spirit of God works in the soul. He had spoken with the Divine authority of one who had Himself seen and known that which He announced respecting the things of God. But Nicodemus had not yet the grace to understand, and so he understood not. In Divine things we can do nothing without grace. We may be able, learned, quick-sighted, intelligent, but without grace we are blind and deaf.

3. Our Lord further tells him that none can speak from direct personal knowledge of heavenly things save He Himself, the Son of Man, and though He had come down from Heaven, He was still present there, in full possession of the Beatific Vision. Happy those to whom Jesus teaches heavenly truths!

Second Week: Friday.
The Brazen Serpent.
St. John iii. 14—21.

Jesus further explains to Nicodemus how the Son of Man must be lifted up upon the Cross, so that all who gaze on Him with faith and love may be saved through Him. He tells how His Mission was to save, not to judge the world. None are condemned, save those who reject and refuse the light, because their deeds are evil.

1. As the brazen serpent was raised up in the desert, and all who gazed with faith upon it were healed of the bite of the poisonous serpents that had attacked them, so the Son of Man was to be exalted on the Cross, that all who believe in Him should not perish, but have eternal life. O merciful Jesus, what a remedy Thou hast provided for the deadly effects of sin ! One look of faith and love on Thee, one cry of mercy from the heart, and all is forgiven !

2. We sometimes are inclined to think of God the Father as our mighty King and stern Master, and of Jesus as praying for us with a gentleness which is in a sort of contrast to the severity of His Father. Not so. God the Father loves the world with the same love as God the Son. He yearns over fallen man with the same Divine yearning. He has the same tender affection for each one of us, the same desire to make us happy to all eternity.

3. Why is it that the Eternal Father does not have this desire fulfilled? Why did the Son shed for so many His Precious Blood in vain? It is because men refuse to listen, hate the light, cling to their own perverse ways. Alas ! have not I often thus feared the light, lest I should be condemned by it?

Second Week: Saturday.
St. John the Baptist's testimony to Jesus.
St. John iii. 23—36.

Some of the disciples of St. John the Baptist, on hearing that Jesus is baptizing and drawing all men to Him, inform their master. St. John declares that the new Teacher is the Bridegroom, the Spouse of His Bride the Church; that it is his own greatest joy to witness the increase of His influence, for He is from Heaven, and the Son of God.

1. Observe how readily and gracefully St. John retires into the background. There is no selfishness and jealousy at seeing how another is preferred before him. On the contrary, to listen to the Voice of the Lamb of God is the fulfilment of all his hopes and his greatest joy. Here is the test of the true Apostle, of the real Saint. He is willing thus to be thrust out of sight and notice. How different from myself, who want to be highly esteemed and noticed!

2. St. John bears witness to the Son of God under a new character, that of the Bridegroom. Thus he declares, under God's inspiration, the fact of the mystical union of Christ and His Church: "He that hath the Bride is the Bridegroom," and so testifies to the Divinity of Jesus. Jesus is the Spouse of each Christian soul. How pure therefore should my soul be if it is to be fit for His sacred presence.

3. St. John further declares that Jesus is from Heaven and teaches what He has Himself seen, and that His words are the words of God, and that all things are given into His hand. If this was true while He was clad in the form of a servant, how much more now that He is King of Kings and Lord of Lords! In His hands then I am always safe.

Third Week: Sunday.
The Well of Samaria.
St. John iv. 1—9.

Our Lord, travelling from Judæa to Galilee, sits down at mid-day, weary and faint, by the well of Samaria. A woman of Samaria comes to draw water, and is astonished that He, a Jew, should ask for water of a Samaritan.

1. Behold the Son of God, thirsty and wayworn, resting during the noon-tide heat. He was wearied out with the journey He had undertaken in order to save man from sin and death. No wonder He is weary with seeking for those who, instead of flocking to Him at the sound of His voice, seem to avoid and shrink from Him. Yet He goes on following them so patiently, so gently calling them. How often have I wearied Him by my obstinacy and my neglect of His voice calling me. *Quærens me sedisti lassus.* Thou hast indeed toiled and laboured to bring me to Thee. O, may I listen and obey!

2. Our Lord begins by asking the woman to do Him a little service. This is often the best possible way of opening up friendly relations with strangers. It creates a kindly feeling on the part of the benefactor, be the benefit ever so small. If there is any one whom I am anxious to gain, I will try and pursue this plan. Men somehow are drawn towards those to whom they are kind.

3. The woman is astonished at the request. The Jews avoided the Samaritans as being apostates from Judaism, unclean, heretics. But where there is a soul to be saved, Jesus sets all else aside. His charity is an all-enduring charity. He came to save the lost, and in this outcast race He recognized many of His elect. Hence I will shun none, despise none.

Third Week: Monday.
The Living Water.
St. John iv. 10—15.

Jesus takes no notice of the woman's wonder, and promises that if she asks of Him, He will give her living water that will spring up to life everlasting, and will make it unnecessary for her to visit the well.

1. "If thou didst know the gift of God!" This was the unfulfilled condition which would be the means of obtaining that living water which satisfies all our needs. If only we recognized the unsearchable value of the gifts of God! If only we appreciated the priceless treasure of His love! If only we knew how eager He is to give us forgiveness, peace, joy, happiness in this life and in the life to come! If only we knew all this, how different our prayers would be, how frequent, how fervent, how persevering! O God, help me to appreciate better the value of Thy gifts.

2. What is the living water which Jesus promises to all who ask for it! It is the gift of the Holy Spirit, that He pours into the hearts of all those who love Him. This gift, like water, cleanses them from all their sins, it refreshes and strengthens them, it nourishes in their souls all the virtues which bud, and blossom, and flourish under the influence of the Holy Spirit indwelling in the soul. Give to me, O Lord, this living water!

3. This living water includes in itself all spiritual delights. It is that of which our Lord promises that He will give us to drink in Heaven freely, and in a measure so abundant as to satisfy all our desires, not drop by drop, as here on earth. It is this living water the sweetness of which this poor Samaritan could not understand, as none can who are still attached to earthly and sinful pleasures.

Third Week: Tuesday.
The True and False Worship.

St. John iv. 16—25.

Our Lord reveals to the Samaritan woman His knowledge of her past life, and in answer to her inquiries about the true God, tells her that it is in the Temple at Jerusalem that He dwells, but that the time was coming when He would be adored all over the world, by those who adore Him in spirit and in truth.

1. See how Jesus, with Divine tact, leads the woman to a confession of her sinful life. He does not blame her, but merely sets before her the sad facts; and grace does the rest. She is not repelled by the implied rebuke, but rather drawn to Him. So, when we tell others of their faults, we shall not repel, but rather attract them, if we speak with something of the charity of Jesus. It is because we are harsh and bitter that they will not listen.

2. The woman then asks Jesus whether it is on Mount Gerizim (as the Samaritans asserted) or in the Temple on Mount Sion, that God was to be worshipped. Jesus gently tells her that it is at Jerusalem that He is to be adored, and that the Samaritans worship an unknown deity. "You adore you know not what." So it is with modern heretics. They bow before their altars, but all is vague and uncertain; they adore they know not what.

3. At the same time, our Lord tells the woman that the time is coming when the worship of the true God will be spread over all the earth. He was thinking of the Catholic Church and its universal sway, and how He would be present, God as well as Man, on every altar, where true adorers would adore Him in spirit and in truth. Thank God that you are one of that happy company.

Third Week: Wednesday.
The Conversion of the Samaritans.
St. John iv. 26—42.

Our Lord declares to the woman that He is the Christ; and on the return of His disciples, who had been buying provisions, the woman leaves her water-pot and hastens to the city, and tells her fellow-townsmen that she has found the Messias. They invite our Lord to Samaria, and He remains there two days, and converts many.

1. The poor woman, conscious of Divine authority in the words of Jesus, remarks that at the coming of the Messias all such difficulties are to be solved, as if already half convinced that it was to Him that she was speaking. Jesus, seeing her growing faith and her honest good-will, reveals to her that He is the Messias, the Deliverer of Israel. The woman listens and believes at once. Do I always show a like docility?

2. No sooner has she given in her allegiance to Jesus, than the disciples arrive with their provisions. She leaves her water-can unheeded, and hurries to the town with her message, that at the well of Jacob is One Who has read her heart, and Who must be the Christ. Admire (1) her eagerness to spread the knowledge of Jesus: (2) her neglect of all else in order to do so: (3) her recognition of His Divine character: (4) the persuasiveness of her earnest words.

3. The Samaritans come forth and invite Jesus to stay with them. O, happy those who issue such an invitation to the Lord of Life! They listen to Him, and He is their Saviour from heresy, and blindness, and sin. Do I recognize Him with similar appreciation when I kneel in His presence, or actually look upon Him, hidden under the sacramental veils?

Third Week: Thursday.
The Ripening Harvest.
St. John iv. 31—38.

During the absence of the Samaritan woman, our Lord tells His disciples that His meat is to do His Father's will, and reminds them of the boundless fields that are whitening for the harvest, ready to be reaped by those who should preach the Gospel of God.

1. Our Lord tells His Apostles, when they press Him to take some food, that He has meat to eat which they know not of. He explains that His food is to carry out, in blind obedience, the task that His Father had laid upon Him. One thing alone He asked Himself: "What is it that My Father wishes me to do?" This is the secret of all sanctity.

2. Jesus directs the attention of His Apostles to the field of work ready for the harvest. It may be that he pointed to the Samaritans, coming in a crowd to hear Him. It may be that He spoke of the great harvest of both Jews and Gentiles. Now, as then, there are fields waiting the reaper. What do I do to help in the harvest? by alms, by my own personal efforts, by training others to work for God?

3. "One man sows and another reaps." How often is this the case! Only in the Day of Judgment will each receive his due share in the work done. A priest receives converts, but he is only the reaper. The sower is some Religious praying in solitude, or some old woman telling her beads. One day sower and reaper will rejoice together. If I cannot reap, at least I can sow, and earn a share in the joy of bringing souls to God.

Third Week: Friday.
The Healing of the Nobleman's Son.
St. John iv. 46—54.

Our Lord, travelling from Samaria to Galilee, arrives at Cana, where a man of authority, belonging to Capharnaum, comes and begs Him to come down and heal his dying son. Jesus tells him to return home, for his son is alive and well. The man believes the word of Jesus, and on his return finds that the boy has recovered at the very moment that Jesus spoke. He and all his home became disciples of our Lord.

1. The ruler of Capharnaum had but a partial faith. He believes that Jesus can cure his son if He is present at his bedside, but it never occurs to him that He can do so equally well from a distance. Yet our Lord does not reject his petition on that account. He loves to fan into a flame even a spark of faith or love. My faith and love is indeed but a tiny spark. O Jesus, fan it into a flame with the breath of Thy grace!

2. Our Lord seems to say to those who listened to Him: "Are not My words enough! Is not the law of love that I publish sufficient to draw your hearts to believe what I speak? No! unless you see signs and wonders you believe not." O Jesus, this shall not be my spirit. No miracles do I need to make me put my trust in Thee, save the miracle of Thy Divine love.

3. The prayer of the ruler is heard, but not in the literal sense. Christ did not go down to his house, but by one word He wrought the cure. So, often He does not grant our prayers as we ask, but eventually He does far better for us. This we should remember when our petitions seem to pass unheeded.

Third Week: Saturday.
The Synagogue at Nazareth.
St. Luke iv. 16—22.

Jesus going into the synagogue at Nazareth on the Sabbath-day, takes the book and reads from the Prophet Isaias (lxi. 1, 2), a prophecy concerning Himself. He tells those present that on that day the prophecy is fulfilled. They wonder at His words, and say: "Is not this the Son of Joseph?"

1. It was the custom among the Jews to assemble every Sabbath-day in the synagogue to read the Law of Moses. Any one present was allowed to read the Law, and to speak on what he had read. Jesus avails Himself of the opportunity thus afforded Him to proclaim His Divine Mission, and reads the passage in Isaias which describes the work that the Messias was to accomplish. How eagerly He is listened to! Something thrills the hearts of those present. They know not that it is God who speaks to them, but they are conscious (1) of the marvellous attractiveness of the speaker; (2) of His Divine authority; (3) of His superiority to all their ordinary teachers. So it always is with those whom God sends. Not so men outside the Church; they may talk beautifully, but they do not touch the heart.

2. What is it Christ proclaims? That He is come (1) to preach the Gospel to the poor, rather than to the rich, (2) to heal the contrite, not the proud, (3) to set at liberty the captive, and those who are crushed with a sense of sin. Ponder on these conditions, and apply them to yourself.

3. Christ declares this Scripture to be fulfilled in Himself. It must have seemed to his hearers a strange boldness in the Son of Joseph the carpenter. Yet He held them spell-bound. They could not resist His gracious words. Can I resist them now?

Fourth Week: Sunday.
A Prophet in His own Country.

St. Luke iv. 23, 24.

Our Lord explains to the people of Nazareth that He is to be rejected in His own country; that He will not perform among them the same signs as elsewhere; and illustrates His intention by the example of Elias and Eliseus, who passed by their own countrymen to carry their message of mercy to strangers.

1. Our Lord tells the Nazarenes that they will expect Him to perform His miracles among them on the principle: "Physician, heal thyself." They forgot that the true relationship to Christ is founded on supernatural charity, not in natural kinship. If I want Him to heal me, I must do His will, for thus I am worthy to be classed as His true mother or sister or brother in the spiritual order.

2. The answer Jesus makes to the thoughts or words of the Nazarenes is the further proverb: "No prophet is accepted in his own country." Why is this? Sometimes it is that the prophet is found out in his home to be but a somewhat ordinary mortal; sometimes (as in our Lord's case) that those who are in continual contact with some teacher of extraordinary holiness, if they are not attracted to him, have their hearts hardened. Sometimes Catholics, religious, even priests, are only hardened by their familiarity with holy things. Alas, that it should be so!

3. Elias in the time of famine was sent to bring plenty to a Gentile; Eliseus healed none of the lepers of Israel, but only a foreign soldier. We must not presume on our being born Catholics, as the Jews did on their belonging to the people of God. God may reject us and bestow His fondest love and best graces on those born and reared outside the Church.

Fourth Week: Monday.
The Anger of the Nazarenes.
St. Luke iv. 25—30.

The Nazarenes, on hearing the words of Jesus, and understanding that He intimated to them that as Elias and Eliseus treated the Jews, so He would treat them, were filled with fury; and seizing Jesus, dragged Him to the edge of a precipice to cast Him down. But He, passing through the midst of them, went His way.

1. What was it that filled the Nazarenes with such fury on hearing the words of Jesus? It was that He gave them to understand that His mercy was not to be bestowed on them or on the Jewish nation. Strangers whom they detested and despised were to be the chief objects of His love. The Son of the carpenter actually declined to make His own city the scene of these wonderful gifts of which He spoke. "Who was this insolent upstart? Were they to suffer His insolence?" Vehement indignation is always a thing to be suspected in fallible man. It is generally a cloak for wounded self-love.

2. These Nazarenes were moved by their pride and hatred of the truth to a crime the guilt of which can scarcely be overstated. They had no excuse. Jesus had dwelt among them for thirty years. They had seen His gentleness, modesty, charity, sweetness. They had heard His words of grace. Yet they rejected and hated Him, and were at heart His murderers. All through pride! He had slighted their dignity. What a lesson for us!

3. Jesus' hour was not yet come, and the maddened crowd of His enemies suddenly missed Him. He had vanished, none knew how. God will protect His own until their work is done. No one really dies before his time,

Fourth Week: Tuesday.
The Call of the Fishermen.
St. Matt. iv. 18—22.

Jesus, leaving Nazareth, goes to dwell at Capharnaum. Walking by the Sea of Galilee, He sees Peter and Andrew fishing, and calls them to come after Him. They immediately leave their nets and follow Him. He afterwards calls John and James, the sons of Zebedee, who obey with similar alacrity.

1. This was not the first time that Jesus had drawn to Himself St. Andrew and St. Peter. (St. John i. 41.) But He had not definitely called them to join Him. He works for the most part gradually in the hearts of men. He sows the seed of His grace, and then He leaves it for a time to mature, and afterwards a second summons leads to willing sacrifice for Him. So He has dealt with me. He has led me on gently, and sought to bring me by degrees nearer to Himself. Have I the good-will of these disciples?

2. Jesus calls these fishermen to be fishers of men, to cast the Gospel net which hauls those who are enclosed in its sacred toils into the rich preserves and the unfathomed waters of the love of God. O what a privilege to be a fisher for God, and to share with Jesus the glorious task of filling the living waters with those who shall bask and shine in them to all eternity.

3. After Peter and Andrew, James and John are called. They are mending their nets with their father Zebedee, when Christ calls them; nets, fishing, father, all count for nought. He calls, and then occupations, possessions. relations, all must be abandoned for His sake. What have I given up for Him?

Fourth Week: Wednesday.
The Synagogue at Capharnaum.
St. Mark i. 21—24.

At Capharnaum, as at Nazareth, Jesus went to the synagogue on the Sabbath-day to listen to the reading of the Law. There happened to be present a possessed person who cried out in terror, and declared Jesus to be the Holy One of God.

1. In the present day, men laugh at the idea of possession, but Holy Scripture teaches its undoubted reality. The spirit of uncleanness is sometimes allowed to inhabit the human body, to control the actions, and speak through the mouths of men, often as the just punishment of long indulgence in sin. Pray God that the devil may never obtain any power or influence over you, as he does in greater or less degree over all who do not resist his evil suggestions.

2. The unclean spirit could not remain silent in the presence of the Son of God. It regarded Him with terror and dismay as its deadliest enemy, and at the same time its Lord. "What have we to do with Thee? Art Thou come to destroy us?" So evil ever shrinks before good. The followers of Jesus are powerful over evil spirits just in proportion as they share His holiness. If we were more like Him, the devil would fear us more, and evil would shrink away abashed in our presence.

3. The devils knew well the holiness of Jesus. They have a natural power to discern the true character of the hearts of men. They cannot read all our inmost thoughts, but they can form a very correct estimate of us; we cannot deceive them as we can deceive men. What a contempt they must have for me! How low must be their opinion of my virtue!

Fourth Week: Thursday.
The Casting Out of the Devil.
St. Matt. i. 25—28.

Our Lord imposes silence on the unclean spirit, and orders it to quit its victim. The devil throws the possessed on the ground in an agony of pain, and then leaves him unharmed. The spectators in awe and amazement ask themselves who this can be who has authority even over the powers of darkness.

1. One word from Jesus, and the unclean spirit is rebuked and holds its peace. How is it, then, that in spite of our appeals to Him, the evil spirits refuse to cease their whispers of temptation, their foul suggestions? It may be because we give them some excuse by our carelessness in not avoiding occasions of sin. It may be that our Lord desires to humble us, and make us feel our weakness and our need of Him. Anyhow, He will give us the graces necessary to resist our foe; and the fiercer the temptation the greater will be our final reward. Courage, then, courage!

2. The devil, when about to go out, tears his victim and throws him on the ground. He will not go out without a struggle. In temptations, the very fact that the repugnance is strongest and the suffering most acute, is often the clearest proof that the devil is about to depart. It is the impotent malice of one who knows that his time is short.

3. When the struggle is over and the devil expelled, the prisoner, freed from his persecution, has suffered no harm. So temptation, however horrible, if resisted, leaves no stain upon the soul; the enemy has harassed and persecuted us, but we have gained strength, not lost it by the conflict. O Christ, may I always bravely resist, and through **Thy word escape unscathed.**

Fourth Week: Friday.
The Healing of Peter's Wife's Mother.
St. Matt. i. 30—33.

On leaving the synagogue, our Lord and His disciples go to the house of Simon Peter, whose wife's mother is lying sick of a great fever. They tell Jesus of it, and He takes her by the hand, and at once the fever leaves her, and she ministers to them.

1. The disciples of our Lord tell Him of the woman who is lying dangerously ill in Simon's house. This is the occasion of her being healed. Our Lord knew of it before, but would He have worked the miracle had they not carried the case to Him? So Jesus waits now for us to tell Him of our needs, and of the needs of those we love. He likes to hear our troubles from our own lips in prayer, and often makes it a condition of delivering us from them.

2. This sick woman had a sort of claim on our Lord on account of her relationship to St. Peter. Jesus would not allow that the Nazarenes had any right to have these miracles wrought amongst them in consequence of His having lived at Nazareth, but this was because they had forfeited their privileges by their incredulity. ' But He recognizes natural ties, and He listens to the prayers of His disciples and friends, and especially of those who have given up all for Him, when they ask on behalf of those who are bound to them by any sort of connection or relationship.

3. One touch of Jesus' hand, and the fever and sickness leave the body of the invalid. It was the practical carrying out of the conviction of another sufferer: " Lord, if I may but touch the hem of His garment, I shall be whole." O Jesus, lay Thy healing hand on me!

Fourth Week: Saturday.
The Work of Jesus at Capharnaum.
St. Mark i. 34—38.

Jesus performed at Capharnaum many miracles, healing the sick and casting out devils, whom He suffered not to speak because they knew Him. In the evening He worked His work of mercy, and very early in the morning He went out into the desert to pray. There His disciples find Him, and when they urge Him to return, He tells them that He is sent to preach in other towns and cities as well.

1. Two kinds of miracles are here recorded of our Lord, the healing of bodily diseases and the casting out of devils. The latter is a far harder task than the former. How reluctant the devil is to quit his victims! Habit almost become second nature. What a firm hold he seems to have on them! So now that the conversion of sinners is a more wonderful exercise of Divine power than the healing of countless diseases.

2. Our Lord would not suffer the devils to proclaim His Divinity. He would not accept the declaration of the truth from such a source as this. So He does not bless the teaching of the truth by wicked men. Their power to influence others seems blighted. The first requisite is not eloquence or learning, but faithfulness to God and the love of Him.

3. In spite of His exhausting labours, Jesus goes into the desert to pray. This was for our sakes: He Himself needed no prayers. But He desired to teach us that when we do a great work for God, or meet with any sort of success, we should before all else go and thank Him, and attribute all to His Divine Providence.

Fifth Week: Sunday.
The Beatitudes: 1. Blessed are the Poor in Spirit.

St. Matt. v. 1—3.

Our Blessed Lord, going up into a mountain, gathers His disciples round Him, and explains to them the Gospel law that He had come to teach to man. He begins with the eight Beatitudes.

" Blessed are the poor in spirit, for theirs is the Kingdom of Heaven."

1. All men desire happiness. We cannot help seeking to attain to it. It is the end and object of our lives. Our Lord's aim in coming down on earth was to teach us how to be happy or blessed. It is of no use seeking to be happy by any other method than by that which Jesus prescribes. O my Lord, teach me this lesson! I desire happiness, and I desire also to learn from Thee the means of attaining it.

2. First and foremost, Jesus places poverty of spirit as necessary to happiness. The world says, "Get rich, and you will be happy," and those who take the advice find that riches do not bring happiness. Jesus says, "Be poor of your own free-will, and you will be happy." The poverty of spirit that He recommends is a detachment from and readiness to resign all we possess for His sake.

3. What does He mean by poverty of spirit? (1) The willing renunciation of such riches as cannot be had without sin. (2) The dependence on God in the use of riches, and the readiness to resign them if we know that He asks it of us. (3) And best of all, the actual renunciation of all possessions, both in will and deed, that we may follow Christ in His sacred poverty. To all such our Lord promises a treasure in Heaven—nay, He says that the Kingdom of Heaven is theirs. What degree have I of this poverty of spirit?

Fifth Week: Monday.
The Beatitudes: 2. Blessed are the Meek.
St. Matt. v. 4.

"Blessed are the meek, for they shall possess the land."

1. Meekness is the outward expression of humility. It is the primary characteristic which our Lord bids us imitate in Himself. "Learn of Me, for I am meek and humble of heart." It is not only the fruit of humility, but the nurse of humility. We continually fail in humility without being conscious of it, but we cannot well fail in meekness without knowing it. We see the effect on others—we hear our own angry words. If, therefore, I wish to be humble, I must cultivate meekness.

2. How beautiful, too, is meekness in itself! Meekness turns away anger; silences the evil speaker; makes men ashamed of their own cruel words; makes us to be conformed to the image of the Lamb of God. Moses was dear to God because he was of men the meekest. "Remember David and all his meekness," says the Psalmist. Our Lord Himself before His enemies was an example of perfect meekness. Alas! how deficient I am in this virtue! Perhaps I even call the meek poor-spirited, and pride myself on my power of self-defence, and my mischievous pugnacity.

3. "The meek possess the land." How true this is even on earth. Men yield to the meek where they would not yield to those who opposed them. The meek are liked and are listened to, and somehow in the end remain masters of the situation. How much more will they be the happy possessors of the heavenly country, the land of God's elect!

Fifth Week: Tuesday.
The Beatitudes: 3. Blessed are they that mourn.

St. Matt. v. 5.

"Blessed are they that mourn, for they shall be comforted."

1. Why is it a blessed thing to mourn? Even in the natural order sorrow chastens and purifies the character. It thus paves the way for supernatural graces. Sorrow, too, under the influence of the Holy Spirit, detaches our hearts from the world, makes us feel our dependence upon God, turns our hearts to Him, makes us long for Heaven. Do not then lament if sorrow overtakes you, but rather rejoice, for "Blessed are they that mourn."

2. Blessed again are they that mourn over their sins. It is the best penance that we can do. But we cannot really mourn over sin unless we have that aversion from it in which purity of heart consists. Blessed too are they that mourn over the sins of others, and are grieved at heart by reason of the manifold offences committed against the Divine Goodness, and of the loss of so many souls dear to the Heart of Jesus. Let us pray for a more heartfelt sorrow for sin. How lightly at present we esteem it!

3. Those who mourn with supernatural sorrow shall surely be comforted. Their consolation is not far away. It will soon pour sweetness into their heart; nay, their very sorrow has in it already an element of sweetness which tells of the joy in prospect and of Heaven to come at last, where in one moment we shall be consoled and compensated for all the mourning of this valley of tears.

Fifth Week: Wednesday.
The Beatitudes: 4. Blessed are they that hunger and thirst after Justice.

St. Matt. v. 6.

"Blessed are they that hunger and thirst after justice, for they shall have their fill."

1. What is it to hunger and thirst after justice? In the case of the sinner, it consists in a longing desire to be freed from his sin, and this is a happy sign of a coming change. So the Prodigal longed after his father's home. So St. Augustine longed to escape from the chain of sin. So the sinner who comes to the tribunal of Penance longs after the blessedness of having the burden of his sins removed. All these are blessed in prospect, not in virtue of their present condition.

2. There is a higher form of this hunger and thirst after justice which is to be found in the Saints in proportion to their sanctity. They are happy, wonderfully happy, happy amid all the trials and sufferings of this valley of tears, but this happiness is the result of their hunger and thirst after the heavenly country. It is the prospect of coming joy that makes them so light-hearted. Is this my case? When I repeat the words, "O Paradise! I would that I were there!" do I mean them, or are they mere empty and unreal sentiment?

3. Those who hunger and thirst after justice shall have their fill. Even in this life the Saints cried out, *Satis, Domine*—"Enough, O Lord," when God poured into their souls spiritual delights. In Heaven all will overflow with joy. The joy that God gives satisfies, but never satiates. We always have enough, yet we never have enough. This is the secret of its sufficiency to all eternity.

Fifth Week: Thursday.
The Beatitudes: 5. Blessed are the Merciful.
St. Matt. v. 7.

"Blessed are the merciful, for they shall obtain mercy."

1. Mercy is the virtue of charity as applied to those who are in distress or trouble. It is the reflection of the love of God for perishing sinners. It is that quality the exercise of which towards ourselves is our greatest need. Without the mercy of God we are lost. Without His mercy we can never free ourselves from sin. Without His mercy we can never hope to see His Face in Heaven. The note of our every prayer should be, "God be merciful to me a sinner!" It is only thus we can hope to be forgiven.

2. To obtain mercy, then, must be the aim of our life. How are we to do so? Christ, the King of Mercy, teaches us the way. We must show mercy to others if we are to find mercy ourselves. It will be in vain for us to cry for mercy, if, when others cried to us in their distress, we turned a deaf ear. Am I thus merciful to others, not from a natural motive, but because I wish to follow in the steps of the merciful and loving Saviour? Or am I severe and hard to my fellow-sinners?

3. What are the methods by which we may show mercy? (1) By mercy to the poor. Daniel tells Nabuchodonosor, "Redeem thy sins by alms-deeds, and thine iniquities by showing mercy to the poor." (2) By tenderness and gentleness to the sick and those in trouble. (3) By forgiving those who have wronged me, as I hope to be forgiven. Are these my characteristics?

Fifth Week: Friday.
The Beatitudes: 6. Blessed are the Clean of Heart.
St. Matt. v. 8.

"Blessed are the clean of heart, for they shall see God."

1. The vision of God is the end of man's existence and the utmost perfection of his happiness. To be shut out from seeing Him to all eternity involves not only the blackness of darkness, but the lowest depth of despair and misery. The enjoyment of all possible earthly pleasures for a million of years would not compensate for the loss of that vision, if only for a moment. The endurance of all possible miseries would be a small price to pay for one instant of the entrancing joy it brings with it. Hence I must frame my life so as to secure this vision of God at any cost.

2. To do this I must fulfil the condition our Lord here lays down. I must be clean of heart. I must never allow my affections to fix themselves on any creature of earth, when I know that in so doing I am acting in opposition to the will of God. I must not indulge any pleasure or passion, however attractive or intense, if I know that God forbids it, else I shall be in danger of forfeiting the vision of God to all eternity.

3. Shall I lose any solid happiness or pleasure by this self-denial? On the contrary, I shall be the gainer even here. I shall earn peace of mind, health of soul and body, cheerfulness, a good conscience; and on earth already I shall begin to taste the happiness of seeing God in such way as is possible during our mortal life. My faith in God and my love of Him will make me despise and hate those gross pleasures which are the husks of swine.

Fifth Week: Saturday.
The Beatitudes: 7. Blessed are the Peacemakers.

St. Matt. v. 9.

" Blessed are the peacemakers, for they shall be called the children of God."

1. The Gospel of Christ involves a strange mixture of peace and war. We have to fight against our spiritual enemies, against our evil passions, against pride and self-will. We are sometimes brought into antagonism with friends or relations for Christ's sake. Yet at the same time Christ is the Prince of Peace, and when we fight against evil, we must always be at peace as far as regards our own dispositions, even with those whose conduct we oppose and condemn.

2. More than this : we must not be content with being ourselves at peace with those around us. We should do all we possibly can to encourage and promote a kindly feeling in the community in which we live. This is within the reach of all, and blessed are those who are thus known as centres of peace. Blessed is the house in which they dwell, for their example is contagious. Am I in this sense a peacemaker?

3. The reward of this peacemaking temper is a recognition of our being children of God, and like to our elder Brother, the Prince of Peace. How beautiful is the footfall of those who thus carry out in their deeds the Gospel of peace. They are dear to the little circle in which their lot is cast. God calls them His beloved children. They are welcome everywhere, and above all will be welcome among the Angels in Heaven.

Sixth Week: Sunday.
The Beatitudes: 8. Blessed are they that suffer Persecution for Justice' sake.
St. Matt. v. 10.

"Blessed are they that suffer persecution for justice' sake, for theirs is the Kingdom of Heaven."

1. To suffer persecution for justice' sake is the common lot of all who follow Christ. It is one of the marks of predestination. As soon as a sinner turns to God, at once some form of persecution or other commences; some kind of suffering is inflicted by those around; sometimes parents disown their child, or a husband changes his former kindness to bitter unkindness; or for justice' sake money, position, worldly influence is forfeited. Blessed are those who here have to endure this persecution for justice' sake.

2. Sometimes God allows His friends to be persecuted and misunderstood, not so much by evil men, or worldly relations, or lax Christians, as by those who are holy and devoted to Him. It has been said that the most cruel form of persecution is that which is inflicted by a holy man, or a Religious Superior. The authority of the persecutor makes the blows he inflicts fall far more heavily; his virtue makes the pain he inflicts far sharper. It is for this reason a very great privilege, only we must be careful that it is for justice' sake, and not because of our pride or obstinacy or carelessness, or other defects, that we are persecuted.

3. What is the reward of being persecuted for justice' sake? None else than the Kingdom of Heaven. The persecuted then will triumph, and their place will be exalted in proportion as they have been thrust low on earth, put out of sight, and cruelly used for conscience' sake. They not only will be admitted into the Kingdom of Heaven, but the Kingdom of Heaven will be theirs.

Sixth Week: Monday.
Christians the Salt and the Light of the World.

St. Matt. v. 13—16.

Our Lord tells His disciples that they are the salt of the world, since by their teaching and example they are to preserve the world from corruption. They are moreover the light of the world, and must let their light shine before men, with the motive of thereby promoting the glory of God.

1. As salt without savour is fit only for the dunghill, so Christians who give bad example are not only useless, but fit only to be cast out and trodden under the feet of men and beasts. This is what has often happened when Catholics have lost their faith and fervour. They have been trodden down by the foot of the persecutor. Pray that you may always spread a savour of good works around.

2. The disciples are, moreover, the light of the world, and from the fact of being Christians, draw the eyes of men upon them. They must not hide their light under a bushel, since God requires of them that they should forward His cause in the world, and promote the love of Him by the brightness of their good example. Ask yourselves if you are in any sense a source of light and happiness to those around you.

3. The Christians are warned by our Lord that in letting their light shine before men, their aim must be to gain glory not for themselves, but for Him. This is the real test of the value of our work. For whom do we do it? If for ourselves, then there is laid up for us not a reward, but the anger of God; if for God, then it will be a source of glory to Him, of good to others, of everlasting joy to ourselves.

Sixth Week: Tuesday.
The Fulfilling of the Law.
St. Matt. v. 21—48.

Jesus came not to abolish the Jewish law, but to carry it on to perfection. Hence He adds to the external mandates of the Jewish covenant a discipline of the heart. It is not sufficient to abstain from revenge and from adultery: the Christian law enforces charity and purity of word and thought as well as of act.

1. The law of Christ includes all the precepts of the Jewish law. Those commandments respecting purity of intention and the absence of thoughts of evil which the Pharisees slighted, our Lord declares to be so important, that whoever shall break one of them deliberately, or teach others to do the same, shall in the Kingdom of Heaven be held of no account, and be thrust out from the presence of God. Are there any precepts of the law of Christ that I think little of or recklessly violate?

2. In old time it was the act of violence that was forbidden. But our Lord says that any one who shall give way to anger or to a desire for revenge in his heart, or say contumelious words to others, shall be liable to the judgments of God. Is not this warning suitable to me, who so often yield to unkind, resentful thoughts, and a desire to take vengeance on those who have offended me?

3. In old time the act of unchastity was forbidden. But Christ reminds His disciples that a deliberate desire is a serious sin against chastity in the sight of God. Am I as careful as I ought to be to avoid all unchaste thoughts and all occasions that are likely to give rise to them?

Sixth Week: Wednesday.
On Alms and Prayers in Public.
St. Matt. vi. 1—13.

Our Lord warns His disciples against giving alms from a motive of ostentation, and against making long prayers in public with the object of being seen and admired by men.

1. If a man gives alms he always receives a reward. If he does it in order to gain human praise, he has the reward he seeks, but from God he receives no reward, but only a punishment for his pride and his desire to gain honour from men. How careful then I must be that when I give alms, it is not done to gain gratitude, or with a desire to be thought highly of, or from mere natural generosity, since thus I gain no reward from God, but, it may be, only call down His anger on me.

2. When we pray in public, or go to Mass when there is no obligation, the thought sometimes comes into our minds that others must be edified by our piety and must admire our devotion. We cannot prevent the thought presenting itself, there is no sin in that, but we must repel it to the best of our ability by dwelling on our own misery, and what we are in God's sight. Such a thought, if indulged deliberately, mars even the most pious prayer, and sometimes takes away all its merit before God, and is an offence, not an honour to Him.

3. Ought we to abstain from prayer, from Holy Communion, from any practice of devotion, because thoughts of vanity come in? Certainly not. Our rule should be to act in the presence of others just as if they were not there. If the temptation to vanity comes, say to the devil with St. Bernard: "I did not begin for you, and I will not leave off for you!"

Sixth Week: Thursday.
On the Laying up of Treasure.
St. Matt. vi. 19—21.

Jesus Christ exhorts His disciples to lay up for themselves treasure in Heaven, not on earth, that their hearts may be where their treasure is.

1. Every one desires to have some treasure to fall back upon in time of need, some resource in the uncertain future. We look forward, and feel the want of something on which to rely for declining years. Our Lord bids His disciples lay up such a treasure, not on earth, where it is perishable and insecure, but in Heaven, for a treasure in Heaven will avail us even on earth. God will not allow those to want who have committed their treasure to Him, and it will earn for us a rich harvest of joy and happiness to all eternity.

2. Men have a love of gathering together riches. They enjoy the activity of it. There is a fascination in it, and the more they have the more they desire. Jesus Christ tells His disciples that they must employ their activity in collecting treasures for Heaven, not for earth. Every act of charity, every prayer, every good thought, every battle against temptation, adds to this eternal treasure. Men who live for God will be astonished in seeing the abundance of the riches they have acquired during life, the inexhaustible wealth they will inherit in Heaven.

3. Our Lord gives another reason for laying up treasure in Heaven. We fix our hearts on what we value most, as our treasure grows, our love for it grows. If we desire to love the things of Heaven, we must lay up our treasure there. O death, how terrible thou art to the man who has peace in his earthly goods! and we may add, How sweet to him who has a rich treasure in Heaven!

Sixth Week: Friday.
On Purity of Intention.

St. Matt. vi. 22, 23.

The light of the body is the eye; the light of the soul is the intention with which we act. If that light be darkness, how great shall that darkness be!

1. The eye it is which directs the movements of the body and determines its aim. So it is the intention with which our actions are done that determines their character and their aim. Two men perform an action externally the same; give an alms, or pay a visit to a friend. One does it for self, the other for God. The act of the former is worthless, or sinful, in God's sight; that of the latter blots out sin, earns grace, and lays up treasure to all eternity.

2. How important then to direct all our intentions to God! We can merit in His sight by all we do. Actions in themselves indifferent—eating, drinking, sleeping, &c.,—all are lighted up with a supernatural light when done for God; and as the whole body is full of light if the eye be single, so our whole life becomes bright before God, if we offer our actions up to Him, and do them for His sake.

3. If our intention be an evil one, our whole life becomes dark in His sight. Actions in themselves most holy become displeasing to God if done from a motive of ostentation, or ill-will, or self-love. O how terrible is the darkness of a soul which is thus actuated by evil motives in things which in themselves seem to be done for God! O my God, save me from this darkness, and grant me the happiness of doing all for Thee!

Sixth Week: Saturday.
On Confidence in God.

St. Matt. vi. 25—34.

The disciples of Jesus are warned by Him against being solicitous about food and raiment, and are invited to trust Him to provide for them. He provides for the birds of the air and the lilies of the field, and He will not let those want who make Him and His justice the end and object of their lives.

1. We are all sometimes harassed by worldly cares. We are in difficulties, and do not see our way out of them. Our means of support are failing us. Those around us do not treat us as they formerly did. We are hindered in our work by unforeseen obstacles, and we are tempted to be discouraged. Such hours it is that test our faith. We may not be able to see our way, and the light may be hidden among the clouds. But at least we can cry out: "O my God, I trust Thee still, I will trust Thee ever. To Thee I commit all my cares, troubles, needs. Forsake me not, O God of my salvation."

2. If God always provides for His children, how is it that we see them miserable, down-hearted, resourceless, discontented? It is because they do not trust Him. It is because they turn their back on Him, and fly to other means of help. They forsake Him, and then complain that He has forsaken them. Have I not sometimes acted thus?

3. There is another reason why we are often thus troubled and disheartened. It is that we do not seek first the Kingdom of God and His justice; we do not regulate our lives as we know God desires, but adopt plans of our own that are not in accordance with what He asks of us. If I desire God to provide for me, I must fulfil this necessary condition.

Seventh Week: Sunday.
On Rash Judgment.
St. Matt. vii. 1—5.

We must not judge others harshly, unless we desire to be similarly judged ourselves. We must not reprehend in others their small defects while we make no effort to correct our own serious faults.

1. The tendency to judge others harshly is one of the strongest of our defects. Conscious of our own short-comings, it would seem as if we should naturally be lenient towards those of others. So far from this being so, we are generally most severe on those defects in others which we ourselves possess. If I am inclined to judge any fault in another severely, it is a sign that in some shape or other the same short-coming exists in me.

2. It is an alarming thought that we shall be judged with the same judgment that we pass on others. If we take a lenient and favourable view of them, God will take a lenient and favourable view of us. If we are severe in our interpretation of their acts, God will in like manner be severe on us. What chance would there be for me if I were to be judged with severity? Shall I not need the most lenient interpretation, and every possible excuse for my countless faults? I will, if only for my own sake, be most lenient to others, and excuse them.

3. There is also a tendency in some natures to play the part of amateur reformers. No one thanks such volunteer and self-appointed critics. They always give offence. They never do any real good. There is one person whom I must reform—myself. I shall not trouble about the trifling mote in my brother's eye, if I pay due attention to the beam in my own.

Seventh Week: Monday.
On the Efficacy of Prayer.

St. Matt. vii. 7—11.

"Ask and it shall be given you; seek and you shall find; knock and it shall be opened to you."

1. The necessity of asking for what we desire to obtain from God is repeatedly urged upon us by our Lord. He knew how the thought would present itself that God knows just what we need far better than we do, and that therefore asking is unnecessary, and so He opposes to this excuse for neglecting prayer, precepts the most urgent and His own example. God is not wont to give good things without prayer. Least of all will He give us any graces unless we ask, and ask earnestly and perseveringly. Is my asking such as is likely to move the Heart of God?

2. In order to enforce this still more, He promises that all who ask shall receive. He reminds us that the father gives good things to His children who ask for them, and that God, whose love for us is immeasurably greater than that of the fondest father for his darling child, cannot refuse good things to us. Dwell on this desire of Almighty God to give to His children all good things that they need, and learn from it great confidence and hopefulness about the future.

3. We must not expect to be heard on our first asking, nor to be heard at all if perchance we are asking for what God sees would be injurious to us. God is trying our patience and resignation to His holy will. But even if we have to wait long, we shall always obtain in the end the fulfilment of every petition which really tends to our true welfare.

Seventh Week: Tuesday.
On Judging by Results.
St. Matt. vii. 16—23.

" By their fruits ye shall know them."

1. It is sometimes said, that we must never judge of the wisdom or rectitude of any course of action by its results, and this is true if we look to immediate results. But the results of any action, or course of action, in the long run is invariably good, if the course of action is good. It must of necessity bring glory to God, and a reward to him who does it. Not at first, but after a time, long or short, its true character will appear in its consequences. Our actions have thus an eternal influence for good and evil.

2. Those who have others under their control always contribute a large share to the after-lives of those whom they have to rule. We find that a holy man sends forth other saints from his school, that the pious mother has children rich in grace. The influence is unconscious, but none the less real. Oh, how happy will those be in Heaven who have thus moulded others to virtue!

3. Jesus tells us that though we must not judge the actions of others, we can nevertheless tell the servants of Christ from the servants of the world or the devil by the work they do as a body. How clearly we see this in the Church as opposed to the sects. In spite of the faults and sins of Catholics, and the great excellencies of many individual Protestants, what a contrast in results ! On the one hand an unbroken tradition of sanctity, on the other an irresistible downward tendency.

Seventh Week: Wednesday.
The House upon the Rock.
St. Matt. vii. 24, 25.

He who listens to the Divine precepts and obeys them, he alone shall enter into the Kingdom of Heaven: he alone has a house upon the rock that no winds or storms can shatter or destroy.

1. Our Lord dwells continually on a criterion of virtue which alone can stand in the Day of Judgment. None will be admitted into Heaven save those whose aim in life has been to do God's will, not their own. They may have been given to much prayer, to alms, to penances. They may have been kind, honourable, generous. They may have preached, prophesied, brought others to God, and even performed miracles; yet if they have followed their own will, not God's, all this will avail them nothing.

2. Only those who thus do the will of God will be able to stand against the storms of persecution, the floods of misery, the whirlwind of temptation. Their natural virtue will succumb, and like a house on the sand, will fall to pieces in the evil day. Nothing will endure save that which is founded on the solid rock of Divine love.

3. But for those who lay as the foundation Christ and Christ alone, who believe in Him, trust Him, love Him, the storms may rage, but not a hair of their head will perish. In every danger those who act under obedience for Christ's sake are in perfect security; nay, every storm and flood and wave only unites them more firmly to the rock on which they rest, Christ Jesus their Lord.

Seventh Week: Thursday.
The Miraculous Draught of Fishes.

St. Luke v. 1—11.

When the crowd pressed around our Lord, He put out to a short distance from the shore in Simon Peter's boat, and thence taught the people. After His sermon He orders the disciples, who had been toiling all night and had caught nothing, to let down their nets. They obey, and enclose a great multitude of fishes.

1. In the absence of Jesus the disciples had laboured, but all in vain. They had thrown their nets, but with no result whatever. So it is with all work in which Jesus is not present. Without Him every work, however pious, is but wasted, and only ends in disappointment.

2. But what a change when Jesus says the word! What is it has changed the fruitless toil into a labour which brings in a rich reward? Three causes—

(1) The net is now cast under obedience. Work done under obedience is always a success. It cannot be otherwise.

(2) Between the fruitless and the successful labour has intervened an act of charity done to Jesus for Jesus' sake. Charity brings a blessing on every work.

(3) The fishermen have meanwhile listened to the sacred words of Jesus, and drunk in something of His Spirit. This sanctifies all work, even the most secular.

3. What was the effect on St. Peter of success? It did not puff him up, but simply humbled him, because he saw it was not his work, but Christ's. This must be my spirit in success, and it will be if I attribute all success to God.

Seventh Week: Friday.
The Healing of the Leper.
St. Matt. viii. 2—4.

A leper comes and adores Christ, saying: "Lord, if Thou wilt Thou canst make me clean." Our Lord touches him, and says: "I will, be thou made clean." And immediately his leprosy is cleansed. Jesus orders him to go and show himself to the priest, and offer the gift commanded by the Law.

1. Leprosy renders the leper an object hideous to behold. It covers his body with loathsome sores, eating away the flesh till the bones appear. It is a fit emblem of sin, which makes us hideous before God. Who is there that is not rendered offensive in His sight by this foul disfigurement? O my God, the foulest leprosy is beautiful compared with my sins.

2. The leper's is a model prayer. Confidence, "Thou canst make me clean," and a strong hope that Jesus intends to cleanse him. We may with advantage make his words our own as we kneel before the Blessed Sacrament. O Jesus my Lord, if Thou wilt, Thou canst make me clean even from sins such as mine; from inveterate habits which nothing but Thy grace can cure.

3. Our Lord with one word cleanses him. So when we make a good act of contrition the guilt of our sin is gone for ever. But though cleansed, the leper still has to show himself to the priest. So the sinner, though his sin may be already forgiven by a good act of contrition, has still to submit himself to the priest in the tribunal of Penance.

Seventh Week: Saturday.
The Healing of the Paralytic.
St. Mark ii. 1—12.

While Jesus was teaching in a house in Capharnaum, four men bring a paralytic, and carrying him to the top of the house, let him down into the midst where Jesus was. He, seeing their faith, said to the paralytic, "Be of good heart, son, thy sins are forgiven thee." To the Scribes who objected to His forgiving sins, He answered by sending away the palsied man perfectly cured.

1. Paralysis represents a different side from leprosy of the nature of sin: the state of utter helplessness to which it reduces the sinner. He can do no work pleasing to God; cannot merit grace or forgiveness; cannot stir a step to be freed from his misery by his own strength or efforts. He is, as it were, dead to all that is good. This is not only the case with mortal sin; even venial sin paralyzes in some degree all that is good in us. Sometimes one little fault, deliberately indulged, seems to take away all our love and all our energy.

2. Observe the trouble the bearers took to bring the paralytic to Jesus. This pleased our Lord; He saw their faith. He likes people who are willing to take trouble. Works of charity which cost us something bring in a rich reward, both to those who do them and those for whom they are done.

3. Why did our Lord first forgive the sin of the paralytic and then heal his sickness? Perhaps because sin was the cause of the paralysis, or to show how the body is unimportant compared with the soul. If you are sick, consider whether it may not be a punishment of sin, and ask yourself how you can make your sickness a real benefit to yourself and a source of glory to God.

Eighth Week: Sunday.
The Vocation of St. Matthew.

St. Matt. ix. 9.

Our Lord, passing by the house where the custom-dues were received, sees Matthew, one of the chief of those who acted as agents of the government in collecting the revenues, sitting engaged in his craft. He simply says: "Follow Me," and leaving all things, Matthew instantly obeys.

1. There is nothing that is so great a snare to a man as a greed of gold. It is a passion that grows with advancing years; it is never satiated. The more a man has, the more he craves for. It has a power to tie the soul to earth more than any other passion. The love of money, says St. Paul, is the root of all evil. Have you a love of money, or at least of getting for yourself the best of everything?

2. Yet the voice of Christ, and the grace He pours into the heart, can overcome even this passion for riches. Matthew loved his money dearly, but when he heard the voice of the Son of God calling him, the heaps of gold lost their bewitching power. He heard a voice within, unheard by those around, which echoed the words of Christ. He saw a hand which beckoned him away. Thus it is when Christ calls. He always gives to the soul a motive impulse which to a man of good-will is simply irresistible.

3. Matthew did not hesitate. Up he got there and then, when he heard that Voice calling unmistakeably. To put off would have been fatal. Learn from him the happiness and necessity of prompt obedience.

Eighth Week: Monday.
The Feast in Matthew's House.
St. Matt. ix. 10—14.

St. Matthew invites Jesus to a feast in his house, and many publicans and sinners came and sat down with Him. The Pharisees are scandalized, but Jesus answers: "They that are in health need not a physician, but they that are sick. I came not to call the just, but sinners to penance."

1. Observe the scene. The Divine Master with that motley crowd gathering eagerly round Him. They are not a class that would be called respectable. Yet how dear they are to Him, and dear by reason of their misery, dear because of their good-will, dear because of the virtue of which they are capable, and to which He desired to raise them. When I am inclined to slight or despise the fallen, I should remember how dear they are to Jesus, perhaps far dearer than I, in my pride and self-sufficiency.

2. See the Pharisees, who are scandalized. They were scandalized because they were themselves so worthless in the sight of God. To be easily scandalized marks a low standard of virtue. To attribute unworthy motives, shows that our motives are of the same kind. I must remember this when I am inclined to take offence and to condemn others. I resemble those Pharisees who were scandalized at the mercy and tender compassion of the Son of God.

3. Jesus came, not to call the just, but sinners. He came to heal the sickness of the soul. This was His mission upon earth; it is His mission still. I am a sinner, a great sinner. O my Lord, I am indeed such, no whole part is in me. O heal me in Thy mercy! If Thou wilt, Thou canst make me clean.

Eighth Week: Tuesday.
The Miracle at the Probatic Pool.
St. John v. 2—9.

At the Probatic Pool at Jerusalem lay a number of sick persons, waiting for the miraculous moving of the water, after which the first person who entered the water was cured. Our Lord, taking pity on a sick man who had lain there for thirty-eight years, bids him take up his bed and walk.

1. The tendency of the present day is to give a natural explanation to all phenomena whatsoever. The sceptic attributes the virtue of all miraculous springs to their medicinal properties. Not so the loyal Catholic; not so any one who believes Scripture is the Word of God; for we read that an Angel descended and the water was moved, and the power to heal was then received. God has the same power now and exercises it. Make a strong act of faith in the continuance in the Church of the power to work miracles.

2. One poor man had been there for thirty-eight years, but never had succeeded in getting into the water first. What a time to wait! Must he not have lost heart? No, he somehow was convinced that he should be cured in the end. And cured he was. God loves the persevering and the confident. Those who trust Him and are willing to wait, and do not desist from their prayers, always get what they ask.

3. This poor man is the type of the inveterate sinner. Sin seems part of his nature, like this man's disease. Yet Jesus can cure it in one moment. Have I some fault that is inveterate? I have had it perhaps for thirty-eight years or more. Still Jesus can cure it. O Jesus, my Saviour, make me whole!

Eighth Week: Wednesday.
The Spirit and the Letter.
St. John v. 10—16.

When the sick man at Jesus' word took up his bed and walked, sound in limb and in perfect health, the Jews were scandalized because this was done on the Sabbath. They asked the man who it was told him to carry his bed, and when they heard it was Jesus, they persecuted Him and sought to kill Him.

1. The sick man, by carrying his bed on the Sabbath, broke the letter of the Law, which forbade the carrying of burdens on the Sabbath. But to blame him for this showed a complete misunderstanding of the precept. None could have urged it, had they not lost the spirit of charity. They read into the precepts of the Law their own hard, unyielding, cruel temper. So, too, I am prone to judge others without considering the circumstances which excuse and sometimes perfectly justify their actions.

2. Notice, too, their unfairness. They asked the man who had been healed, not who it was that had healed him, but who it was that had told him to carry his bed. They overlooked the miracle of mercy, and fastened on the point where they thought they could find fault. This is the spirit against which our Lord warned His disciples, " Judge not." It is blind to the good in a man's conduct, but has a keen eye to the supposed evil.

3. See the result of this habit of rash judgment. They persuaded themselves that they ought to punish and even put to death one who broke the Law. This sort of righteous indignation is too common now, and we indulge it against those who do not fall in with our notions, and we fancy that we are zealous for God.

Eighth Week: Thursday.
The Corn-plucking on the Sabbath.
St. Matt. xii. 1—8.

As our Lord and His disciples passed through the corn-fields on the Sabbath, His disciples began to gather the ears of corn and to eat them. The Jews again are indignant, and again Christ rebukes them.

1. It is the law of the Catholic Church that ecclesiastical precepts do not hold in case of grave inconvenience. This is confirmed by our Lord's words on this occasion. The disciples were not bound by the Law that forbade the gathering of corn on the Sabbath, because the Law did not really apply to the case of hungry men. Learn to be wide and liberal in interpreting the Church's laws for others.

2. Our Lord defends His disciples by parallel cases from history. Holy men broke the ecclesiastical law in case of necessity. The priests in the Temple break the Sabbath and are blameless. When we are inclined to condemn others we shall generally find some case in the lives of the Saints when a Saint acted just in the same way as those we are judging thus rashly.

3. Jesus gives as the reason which justified the disciples that God desires mercy and not sacrifice. The disciples had been so busy with works of mercy that they had had no time to eat. "Blessed are the merciful, for they shall obtain mercy." Dearer to the Heart of Jesus are works of charity done for His sake, than a mere punctilious observance of ecclesiastical usages. Nothing like mercy! He who is merciful will obtain not only mercy but everything else He needs from God.

Eighth Week: Friday.
The Jews rebuked.
St. John v. 16—47.

The indignation of the Jews against Jesus for working miracles on the Sabbath was roused to fury when He declared to them that God was His Father, and implied that He was equal to God. He reproves them by reasserting His own Divine power.

1. How was it that the Jews were so inexcusable for rejecting our Lord? It must have startled them to hear Him asserting His Divinity, and one might have fancied that they might be pardoned for refusing to believe. Their guilt lay in the self-caused blindness which would not or could not recognize His holiness, and the Divine loveliness which shone through His every word, work, and look. In face of this nothing could excuse them. So with all who are really brought face to face with the Catholic Church, and have a sufficient opportunity of recognizing its supernatural beauty. They, like the Jews, are inexcusable.

2. Our Lord's defence of Himself is that His Father still works on the Sabbath, creating, preserving, co-operating with every creature throughout the world. On Him no law is imposed because He is Lord of all. The Only-Begotten Son of God must needs do what His Eternal Father does, and therefore as God the Father works hitherto so also the Son of God. Hence our Lord clearly asserts His Godhead, and so the Jews understood it. Make an act of faith in this unity of action of the First and Second Persons of the Blessed Trinity.

3. Our Lord goes on to say that he who honoureth not the Son honoureth not the Father who sent Him. So those who fail in honour to the Saints and to the Holy Mother of God fail in honour to Christ and to God. What is my practice in this matter?

Eighth Week: Saturday.
Our Lord retires before His Enemies.
St. Matt. xii. 14—21.

The Pharisees hold a consultation among themselves how they may destroy Jesus. In order to avoid their malice, He retires to the Sea of Tiberias, but is followed thither by a great multitude of people.

1. The miracles worked by Jesus on the Sabbath-day rouse the anger of the Pharisees, and they plan his Death with the Herodians. It seems strange that they could withstand the beauty of His Divine charity. But the Pharisees were proud, and pride looks askance at every good work which threatens to diminish its own dominion and raises a rival. Against this spirit we must be on our guard. One who loves God rejoices in all the good done by others, even though it interferes with his own supposed privileges or rights.

2. It was those in authority and those who had the greatest influence with the people who were our Lord's bitterest opponents. What could be more fatal in all appearance to His chance of success than this? Yet it was a sign of His future triumph. He desired to teach us that every great work for God is sure to meet with strong opposition and discouragement at first, often from those in authority, and so to cheer us amid difficulties.

3. Our Lord could have silenced or defeated His enemies in a moment. But He knew that it was His Father's will that He should simply retreat before His opponents, so He fled as if He feared their violence. So now Christ often appears unable to cope with those who hate Him and the Church He has founded. We must wait to the end before we can understand the ways of God.

Ninth Week: Sunday.
The Enrolment of the Apostles.
St. Luke vi. 12—16.

After a night spent in prayer, our Lord chose the twelve Apostles to be with Him, that He might send them to preach and to heal sickness and cast out devils. Of these Simon is the first; to him Jesus gives the name of Peter.

1. Our Lord before the choice of the Apostles, spends the whole night in prayer. He had no need to pray, but He prayed that He might set us an example. He desired to teach us that before we take any important step in life we should pray, and pray with perseverance. How many follies we should avoid, how much misery we should escape, if only we prayed more and commended our every action to God, instead of following our own natural impulses, and the suggestions of mere human prudence.

2. Our Lord chose His Apostles; they did not choose Him. He said to them afterwards: "You have not chosen Me, but I have chosen you." Jesus must make the choice of us if we are to do any work for Him that will be valuable to eternal life. All men have a vocation. There is some line in life that our Lord has chosen for each, if they will but follow His call. Some He calls to the cloister; some to a life in the world; some to be married, some to be single; some to be men of business, lawyers, doctors, priests, &c.

3. The choice had for its main object that they might be with Him, His friends, companions, fellow-workers, loving and loved by Him. To this it is that God calls all. God intends my life, my profession, to bring me nearer to Jesus, that I may be with Him both in this world and in the next.

Ninth Week: Monday.
The Sermon on the Plain.
St. Luke vi. 17—26.

After this choice of His Apostles our Lord comes down on to the plain, and there delivers a sermon to the assembled multitude. It differs from the Sermon on the Mount in being delivered, not to His disciples only, but the crowd at large. Among other points of difference, it adds to the Beatitudes several solemn warnings.

1. "Woe to you that are rich, for you have received your consolation." When our Lord uses this word *woe*, it implies a terrible judgment to come. He tells the rich that they "have received their consolation," and clearly implies that there is little consolation for them hereafter. We may not perhaps be rich, but even those who have not riches sometimes have the spirit of the rich in their selfishness and attachment to earthly things. Woe to us if we thus cling to anything on earth.

2. "Woe to you that are filled, for you shall hunger." There are some persons who seem to get all that makes life comfortable. They are satisfied, content with themselves, and have no appreciation of the miseries of this valley of tears. We are inclined to envy them, but to such our Lord says, Woe!

3. "Woe to you when men shall bless you." This seems at first at variance with the duty of seeking to please all and to win all. But what our Lord denounces is the hunting after human applause and the intoxication of worldly success. Those who live for God always meet with opposition. They are sure to be misunderstood, blamed, thwarted, reproached. How much happier is this than to hear the applauding shouts of the crowd!

Ninth Week: Tuesday.
The Centurion's Servant.
St. Luke vii. 1—10.

A Roman centurion, who had been most friendly to the Jews, had a servant dangerously ill. When he heard of Jesus, he sent the ancients of the Jews to Him, to beg Him to heal his servant. Afterwards he sends a number of his friends, telling Christ that he was not worthy of His presence in his house, and entreating Him to say the word and heal the servant. Jesus, admiring his faith, heals him at once.

1. The love of the Roman centurion for the Jews and his kindness to them was the preparation for his becoming a servant of Jesus Christ. The Jews alone possessed the true faith. This centurion must have been a lover of truth, and this love led him to love those who were in possession of the truth. We ought to remember that Catholics are, far more than the Jews were, the chosen people of God, and we are bound to love and honour them for their Master's sake.

2. The centurion was also a humble man. He declared himself unworthy that our Lord should come under his roof. How different from Naaman, who was offended because Eliseus did not treat him with pomp and ceremony. How different from Simon the Pharisee, who thought he was doing our Lord a favour in inviting Him to his house. Our Lord loves such simplicity; it is the surest sign of solid virtue.

3. These words of his, *Domine, non sum dignus*, are adopted by the Church for those who approach the Blessed Sacrament of the Altar. Say them often to God, not only at Holy Communion, but on every occasion. Say them now: Lord, I am unworthy, unworthy of all Thy goodness!

Ninth Week: Wednesday.
The Widow of Naim.
St. Luke vii. 11—16.

As Jesus entered the little town of Naim, He met the funeral procession of the only son of a poor widow. Moved with compassion, He said to her, "Weep not," and straightway bade the young man arise.

1. Jesus was entering Naim with His disciples and a great crowd. But He does not therefore pass by unheeded the poor broken-hearted mother, who had lost her only son. See how tenderly He accosts her: "Weep not." He is sorrowful at seeing her sorrow. He longs to comfort her. He addresses to her words that of themselves lift half the weight of sorrow from her heart. Jesus is still the same, still so full of compassion, so kind, so tender-hearted. He does not overlook our sorrows, and He will comfort us erelong, and say, Weep not! Be not dejected. Do not I love you with a Divine love?

2. His compassion does not end with words. He stops the bier, and bids the dead man arise, and gives him back to his mother in perfect health. So now He listens to the mother's silent prayer, and watches for the mother's tears. How many a son dead to God has been restored by his mother's tears and prayers! Weep not then, O sorrowing mother! Jesus will bid your son arise.

3. On all there came a great fear. God was in their midst, and they trembled at the thought. So in our midst He dwells in the Blessed Sacrament. Have we the same filial fear for Him, the same loyal affection, the same reverence for the place where He dwells?

Ninth Week: Thursday.
The Visit of St. John's Disciples.
St. Luke vii. 17—23.

St. John, finding that some of his disciples doubted whether Jesus were the Messias, sends them to see for themselves. Our Lord points to the works that He was performing, and bids them judge from these.

1. When the disciples of St. John asked him whether the Prophet of Galilee were the promised Messias, he did not answer them directly, but bid them inquire for themselves. This is the way to lead men to the Truth. Bring them face to face with it, let them see its results and the wonders it works, and then, if they are men of good-will, they will have no difficulty in recognizing it.

2. When our Lord in His turn is asked the same question by the messengers John sent, He in the same way gives no direct answer, but in their presence heals diseases, opens the eyes of the blind, and casts out devils. Here is the test of Truth and of the teachers of Truth. Have they remedies for our spiritual diseases? Can they cast out the devils of malice and impurity and selfishness and pride? Compare the Catholic Church in this respect with sectarian bodies, and recognize in it the religion that comes from God.

3. The final test given by our Lord of a teacher sent from God, is, that he preaches to the poor. This love of the poor is a great mark of love to Jesus. A dislike for them is a bad sign. Do I love the poor for Jesus' sake?

Ninth Week: Friday.
Our Lord's witness to John the Baptist.
St. Luke vii. 24—28.

Jesus, when John's disciples had departed, speaks of him to the multitude. He describes him as a prophet and more than a prophet, so that of all the prophets there had been none greater than he. Yet in the Kingdom of Heaven One had arisen greater than John.

1. Our Lord first tells the multitude what John is not. (1) He is no reed shaken by the wind. Inconstancy is fatal to holiness. Self-will and pride always make a man unstable. (2) He is not one of those clothed in luxurious garments. Such men are the friends of kings, not of God. The true prophet loves coarse raiment and hard fare. Apply these tests to yourself, and judge whether you have any of the spirit of the prophet and saint in you.

2. Our Lord next tells them what St. John really is. A prophet and more than a prophet; the Angel sent before the face of God, one with whom none of the other prophets can be compared. What a magnificent eulogium! How had St. John earned it? (1) By his humility. (St. John i. 27.) (2) By his abstinence. (St. Matt. iii. 4.) (3) By his love of solitude and prayer. (St. Luke i. 80.) Do you deserve the praise of Christ for holiness by these means?

3. The special privilege reserved to St. John was that he was to be the Angel or Messenger who was to prepare the way for Christ. If we cannot preach the Gospel, we can at least prepare the ways of God; we can win those around us by our charity, our patience, our constant fidelity, and can prepare them to receive the good seed of the Word of God.

Ninth Week: Saturday.
The Result of neglected Graces.
St. Matt. xi. 20—24.

The cities where most of our Lord's miracles had been performed had rejected the graces offered them. He declares that in the day of Judgment it will be more tolerable for the heathen cities of Tyre and Sidon, and for the wicked Sodom and Gomorrha, than for the cities which through pride had turned aside from the Son of God.

1. "Woe to thee, Corazin! Woe to thee, Bethsaida!" Yet these were places which had enjoyed the privilege of being the scene of our Lord's most wonderful works. Yet to them—woe! Is not this enough to frighten us, when we think how many wonderful works He has done for us? We have indeed cause to tremble lest He denounce woe to us.

2. We sometimes congratulate ourselves on our graces and privileges, and we do so rightly. But we are prone to forget that every grace carries with it a corresponding responsibility, and that if we do not avail ourselves of it, it will not leave us as we were before we received it, but in a far worse condition. We shall have turned God away from us, and even if we have not actually sinned, we shall have rendered Him less ready to give us graces for the future.

3. How is it that men reject graces? Sometimes through indolence, sometimes through self-love, sometimes through cowardice, sometimes and most often through pride. Grace demands submission. "He giveth grace to the humble," and men hate to humble themselves. Examine why you have forfeited so many graces.

Tenth Week: Sunday.
The Divine Consoler.
St. Matt. xi. 26—30.

Our Lord thanks His Eternal Father for hiding the mysteries of God from those who think themselves wise and prudent, and revealing them to the little ones and the humble of heart. He calls on all who labour and are burdened to come to Him and be refreshed; to take upon them His sweet yoke and light burden if they desire rest to their souls.

1. Natural ability and human learning do not qualify him who possesses them for an insight into supernatural truth, unless they are accompanied by humility of heart. If you would have a deep knowledge of God, you can only obtain it by being humble of heart, and by praying the Son of God to reveal to you those hidden truths which our unassisted intellect fails to grasp.

2. We are also apt to think that troubles and sorrows are an evil in life. Yet how many have been brought to Jesus by a consciousness of their own misery, who, if all had gone prosperously, would have gone on in their pride and self-satisfaction to their own destruction. Thank God if you are thus humbled: when trouble presses hard, listen to Jesus saying, "Come unto Me, ye who labour and are burdened, and I will refresh you."

3. The Eternal Son of God chooses two special characteristics in which we must imitate Him, if we are to find a lasting peace: *meekness* and *humility*. The absence of these is the cause of all our disquiet and discontent. If we willingly take His yoke upon us, and try to be meek and humble, we shall soon find a delicious peace, rest, and tranquillity in our souls.

Tenth Week: Monday.

The Conversion of St. Mary Magdalen.

St. Luke vii. 36—50.

In the house of Simon the Pharisee, Mary Magdalen the sinner approaches Jesus while He is sitting at table, and with many tears kisses His sacred Feet in token of her contrition and love, and anoints them with a box of precious ointment. Jesus forgives her sins, dismisses her in peace, and contrasts her devotion with the coldness of His entertainer.

1. While we read that thousands and tens of thousands came to Jesus to be healed of their bodily infirmities, Mary Magdalen is the only one who is recorded to have come to Him for the cure of the sickness of her soul. So now there are many who pray most earnestly for earthly blessings, but there are few who with the same energy pray for advance in virtue and greater love for God. Yet how miserable are all the advantages of this world compared with the least progress in love of God and purity of heart! If only we knew the gift of God, we should ask for the living water of spiritual graces.

2. Our Lord not only granted Magdalen's request and healed her soul, but raised her at once to a high level of holiness. Her devotion to Him was in proportion to her former sins. "Many sins are forgiven her, for she hath loved much." Why should not I come to the feet of Jesus, and so earn a like blessing?

3. Mary did not come without a gift, and a gift of the best she had. This was at the same time a proof of her love and the cause of her success. Nothing wins the Heart of Jesus like generosity.

Tenth Week: Tuesday.
The Blasphemy of the Pharisees.

St. Matt. xii. 22—37.

On the occasion of our Lord's healing one who was possessed with a devil, and was thereby rendered blind and dumb, the Pharisees accused Him of casting out devils through Beelzebub, the prince of the devils. Our Lord refutes their wicked calumny, and points out the contradiction that would be involved in Satan casting out Satan.

1. The person who was brought to our Lord had been deprived of sight and hearing by the devil dwelling within. Satan does not work such effects now in those who are subject to his power. But he deprives them of spiritual sight, and makes them blind to the truths of faith, deaf to the inspirations of the Holy Spirit, and dumb in the presence of God. Ask yourself whether in your heart dwells any evil influence which thus comes between you and God.

2. When our Lord casts out the evil spirit and restores its victim to his senses, the Pharisees blasphemously declare that it is through the power of the devil that it has been driven out. This was the lowest depth of that malice that attributes an evil source to a holy action. Have I not sometimes shared this malice when I have judged unkindly of the servants of God, and put a bad interpretation on what they do?

3. Jesus deigns to refute his calumniators by argument. He appeals to facts and to reason. Could evil be cured by the evil one? Could the devil be so foolish as to expel his own? It is one of the proofs of the truth of the Church that, among all the various religions in the world, she alone can expel the evil one from the souls of men.

Tenth Week: Wednesday.
The Sin against the Holy Ghost.
St. Matt. xii. 31, 32

Our Lord declares that every sin shall be forgiven to men except blasphemy against the Holy Ghost, which shall not be forgiven either in this world or in the world to come.

1. What is meant by the sin against the Holy Ghost? It is the wilful, deliberate, open, persistent denial of the known truth. One who perseveres in this, and does not retract his blasphemous words, shuts the door of the Kingdom of Heaven against himself. Grace cannot enter his heart. He is already among the reprobate. This is the sin of the founders of heresies, of such men as Arius and Nestorius and Luther. Make an act of faith in the known truth of the Catholic Church by way of reparation for the blasphemies of heretics.

2. Why is this of all sins the deadliest? Because it approximates most nearly to the spirit of Satan, who was a liar from the beginning. Because it is a sin, not of weakness, but of unmixed pride. Because it is a direct and deliberate outrage and insult to God, and a spurning of the Spirit of Love. Because its root is hatred of God, so that he who commits it would, if possible, drag God from His throne in Heaven, and sit there in His place. Make an act of submission to God, and detest the pride that rebels against Him.

3. All other sins can be forgiven to men. As long as there is not this rebellion in the heart, grace can find its way in, and even the greatest sins can be forgiven. Thank God for His unspeakable mercy, and have great confidence that He will forgive all your sins when you pray to Him with a humble heart.

Tenth Week: Thursday.
Idle Words.
St. Matt. xii. 33—37.

"Out of the abundance of the heart (says our Lord) the mouth speaketh. A good man out of a good treasure bringeth forth good things, and an evil man out of an evil treasure bringeth forth evil things. But I say to you that every evil word that men shall speak, they shall render an account of it in the Day of Judgment. For by thy words thou shalt be justified, and by thy words thou shalt be condemned."

1. Nothing gives a truer clue to our character and to the extent of our virtue than our words. We talk away on all sorts of subjects, and through our conversation there shines forth before our hearers what we really are. What sort of impression do I leave among those with whom I converse? Do my words tend to raise and edify them.

2. For every idle word we shall have to render an account. This does not mean that we shall be severely judged for playful words, or words of harmless pleasantry, words which came out as it were spontaneously from the innocent fulness of our heart. These are only idle words when they cannot possibly serve any good purpose. It is the ill-natured story, the cutting or sarcastic remark, the rather indelicate anecdote, which we shall have reason to regret at the Judgment. These it is which are idle words and often worse.

3. When our Lord says that by our words we shall be justified or condemned, He does not mean to exclude deeds or thoughts. He means that apart from all else our words will be sufficient to earn the approval or condemnation of our Judge. **Can I stand this test?**

Tenth Week: Friday.
True Relationship to Christ.
St. Matt. xii. 47—50.

While Jesus is teaching, His Mother and His brethren are announced as desiring to speak with Him. He looks round on His disciples, and declares that there is a relationship nearer to Him than the relationship of blood, and that it consists in a perfect conformity to the will of His Father in Heaven.

1. The Catholic Church is the true family in the supernatural order. All who belong to it are brethren one to another, and brethren of Jesus Christ. The union between every soul which is in a state of grace and Jesus Christ is far closer than any possible earthly union. His love to it is incomparably greater, and He watches over it with a care far surpassing that of the fondest mother; listening with interest to all that concerns it, ready to help in time of need, providing with loving care for all its wants. Think how dearly Christ loves you, and be comforted thereby.

2. In this spiritual relationship none is so closely united to Jesus as His holy Mother. The spiritual union between His soul and hers, by reason of her perfect conformity to the will of God, was far closer than that which united her to Him as her Son. This latter, wondrous privilege as it was, was quite subordinate to the privileges to which she attained by reason of her answering obedience to every grace.

3. Jesus has for us all the devotion of the most loving of brothers and the most affectionate of sons. His love embraces every possibility of affection, and every beauty and tenderness that is possible in human love. Alas! how faint is my love to Him, compared with His love to me.

Tenth Week: Saturday.
The Sower and the Seed.
St. Matt. xiii. 1—9.

The Parable of the Sower was explained by our Lord Himself to His Apostles. We have therefore no need to search for the application of His sacred words.

1. The Sower is the Son of Man, and subordinately to Him, His ministers, bishops, priests, all faithful Christians who speak for God. But it is always Christ our Lord who speaks through their mouth, even if their utterances be the most imperfect. He makes use of imperfect means as the channels of His graces. What reason, then, have we to attend to His warning: Take heed how ye hear! It is Christ who speaks through the mouths of men; we must hear not carelessly, not critically, not as judges, but humbly, in the spirit of little children, and with a desire to learn something for ourselves.

2. The seed is the word of God. It takes various forms: Holy Scripture, pious books, sermons, good conversation, the whispers of our Guardian Angel, holy thoughts. But in each case it is the word of God, and therefore infinitely precious, and intended by Him to bring forth fruit to eternal life.

3. The field is the world and every human heart. Christ scatters the seed, not only amongst those in the Church, though for them it is much more abundant, but among all heretics, Jews, Pagans, Mohammedans. In every heart the fructifying seed is sown, and graces enough and more than enough to nourish it. Hence none are excused by ignorance, and least of all the children of the Church.

Eleventh Week: Sunday.
The Roadside and Stony Ground
St. Matt. xiii. 20, 21.

Our Lord describes the hearts of men as corresponding to four kinds of ground. (1) The wayside. (2) Rocky ground. (3) Thorny ground. (4) Good ground.

1. The wayside, where the seed is at once carried off by the birds of the air, corresponds to the hardened heart, whence the devil carries away each inspiration or holy thought without its ever sinking into the soul. Those thus hardened are of all the most hopeless. Sin repeatedly indulged has almost taken away the power of hearing the voice of God. Pray earnestly that you may never fall into such a condition as this.

2. The rocky ground, where, beneath a slight covering of earth lies a hard, stony rock, is the soul of one who has good impulses and acts on them. But he has not a firm good-will, and soon wearies of the yoke of Christ. His love for good things is a surface love; he has not counted the cost of serving God. Beware of that impulsive action which begins some good work with excited eagerness, but soon flags and fails.

3. The noonday sun scorches up the shallow-rooted plant. So trials, and difficulties, and hardships, and disappointments, destroy the zeal and energy of one who is not deeply rooted in the service of God. It is the time of trial that tests our good-will. When the noonday heat oppresses, then may be seen whether we persevere.

Eleventh Week: Monday.
The Thorny Ground.
St. Matt. xiii. 22.

1. The thorny ground in some respects seems to offer a better chance to the seed sown in it than the rocky ground. When the seed is cast all looks fair: the ground is deep, the thorns are hidden. All goes well for a time, the seed takes root and promises to flourish. But as time goes on the thorns grow up and finally prevent the seed sown from bringing forth any fruit. So the grace of God often takes root in the soul, and there is every prospect of the fruits of holiness springing up in abundance. But after all the sprouting seed is choked up by the evil influences around.

2. What are these influences? (1) Love of riches. A man gets fond of money, and makes it the first object in his life. (2) The cares of this world. He allows other interests to come before the interests of God; his friends, his position, his influence, his popularity, are put first and his duty to God second. (3) The pleasures of life. Not necessarily sinful pleasures, though these most effectually choke the word, but the round of fashionable amusements, the enjoyments and gaieties of society. O how many have been ruined by these! Have not I good cause to fear lest they in some form or other hide God from me?

3. Is it possible to be att'ched to these and to serve God at the same time? No, for no man can serve two masters. God is a jealous God. Woe to me if I allow any of these thorns to choke the holy inspirations of God. O death, how terrible thou art to the man who has peace in his possessions!

Eleventh Week: Tuesday.
The Good Ground.
St. Matt. xiii. 8, 23.

" He that receiveth the seed on good ground, this is he that heareth the word and understandeth and beareth fruit, and yieldeth the one an hundred-fold, another sixty, and another thirty."

1. If we are to bring forth fruit to eternal life, the first thing necessary is that we should understand the word that is sown in our hearts. This gift of understanding is not a mere matter of the intellect, it is a grace which is given to men of good-will. Two men of like intelligence read a passage of Holy Scripture; it makes a lasting impression on one and not on the other. The reason is that one has a good-will, and so God gives the grace without which all spiritual things are hidden from us. The other has not the same good-will, and so he fails to comprehend it. Hence, whenever you read the word of God, pray for a good-will, and grace, and light.

2. It is not enough to understand unless action follows, and the seed sown leads to good works; done for the love of God and under the influence of the Holy Spirit. This is the real mark of predestination, to persevere in obedience, not to be beaten back by difficulties, not to be turned aside by the attractions of the world. Have I this perseverance, without which we cannot bear good fruit?

3. Different plants bear a different amount of produce, some an hundred-fold, like the saints of God; some sixty, like ordinary good men; some thirty, like those who are imperfect Christians. Yet happy all who bear good fruit! God grant that I may be of their number!

Eleventh Week: Wednesday.
The Parable of the Cockle.
St. Matt. xiii. 24—28; 36—50.

In this parable our Lord compares the Church to a field in which good seed has been sown, but during the night an enemy comes and oversows it with cockle. The servants want to pull up the cockle, but the master orders that both should be left till the harvest.

1. The Parable of the Cockle is a great consolation to us if we are inclined to be astonished and cast down by the amount of evil that is to be found in the Church of God. So many wicked men! So much indifference, worldliness, selfishness, ambition, to say nothing of more serious sins. Can this be the Spouse of Christ? Yes, and the very existence of the evil is but the carrying out of what the Master had foretold.

2. The reason given by the master why the cockle should not be rooted up is that we cannot always discern wheat from cockle until the harvest-time. They are so alike! Hidden pride has all the look of exalted virtue, and exalted virtue is sometimes unattractive to men, and misjudged by them. Learn never to judge any one, lest you condemn one who is dear to God.

3. At the Judgment there will be no doubt as to what is cockle and what is wheat. In every action that I have ever done the good will be clearly discerned from the evil and the indifferent. When I examine even my best actions, how few there are that are nought else but good grain fit for the Master's table! How much cockle! How many imperfections! How many even of venial sins!

Eleventh Week: Thursday.
The Seed cast into the Ground.
St. Mark iv. 26—29.

In this parable our Lord compares the Kingdom of God to seed cast into the ground, which sprouts and grows up gradually, as it were of its own accord, until at length, when it is ripe, the sower puts in the sickle because the harvest is come.

1. In this parable the Kingdom of God is the grace falling on good ground. For a long time its effects are scarcely perceptible, but nevertheless it is gradually growing up, first the blade, then the ear, then the full corn in the ear. Sometimes we fancy that we make no progress, that we were better in past years than now. But we need not fear. The good work is going on in us though we are not conscious of it, and one day we may hope to be gathered ripe into our Master's harvest.

2. Observe that the process is a gradual one. Men do not become saints all at once. At first there is but little sign of their holiness. They have many faults and imperfections. We must not expect of ourselves or of others perfection in a week. Sometimes God leaves in His saints some manifest defect for long years. They are ripening for the harvest, and even now it may be, are bearing far more fruit than us.

3. The earth of itself brings forth the fruit when once it has received the good seed. So no grace that God gives us, no trial that He sends us, no sickness, calamity, poverty fails of producing fruit to eternal life if it is received in the heart of a man of good-will. Often his only part in the process is that he acquiesces in the will of God and does not rebel, and out of this there comes great fruit to the glory of God.

Eleventh Week: Friday.
The Parable of the Mustard-Seed.
St. Matt. xiii. 31, 32.

Our Lord compares the Kingdom of Heaven to a mustard-seed, which is the least of all seeds, but grows up into the mightiest of trees.

1. The Kingdom of Heaven here primarily signifies the visible Church of Christ. How feeble are its beginnings! At Pentecost only a handful of obscure Jews, mostly of the lower class rough, uneducated, with no special talents. How wonderful its growth! It gradually conquered the world, and that in spite of persecution without and treachery within in spite of whole nations that revolted from its yoke, in spite of the worldliness and lukewarmness and tepidity of its children, it is still firm and strong as ever. Make a firm act of faith in the indefectibility of the Church of Christ.

2. The birds of the air come and take shelter in the branches of it. All those who fly heavenwards shelter themselves under the shadow of the Catholic Church. If they do not recognize her as their true home, it is only because owing to their special circumstances she is so far away that their eye cannot recognize her glories. But whenever the Catholic Church is well discernible, none ever turn away from her if they are winging their way to the Heavenly City.

3. In her branches all these denizens of heaven take shelter from the noonday heat, from storm and tempest, from persecution and suffering, from toil and labour. They find rest and refreshment in the virtues of her saints, in the sacraments, in the sweet consolations that God gives through her to the souls that He loves.

Eleventh Week: Saturday.
The Treasure hid in the Field.
St. Matt. xiii. 44.

"The Kingdom of Heaven is like unto a treasure hidden in a field, which a man having found, hid it, and for joy thereof goeth and selleth all that he hath and buyeth that field."

1. It seems at first a contradiction that the Kingdom of Heaven should be compared sometimes to a city set upon a hill, conspicuous before all men, sometimes to a hidden treasure which is known and prized only by a few. The Church of Christ cannot be ignored even by those who hate it the most. Its existence is obvious to the world; but its countless perfections and the happiness of being one of its members are hidden from all save those who have in their hearts the love of God, and the desire after Him. To me, O Lord, unfold the beauties of Thy spotless Spouse, that I may love her as I ought.

2. This treasure must be purchased; it cannot be had for nothing. A price must be paid by those who would possess it, and often a heavy price. Hence the trials and sufferings of all who would serve God, or who aim at perfection. Hence the worldly troubles which often overtake those who are converted to the faith, and the sacrifices that are required of them. Happy they who joyfully pay the price for this priceless boon.

3. The man who finds this treasure hides it. He does not proclaim to the world at large the joy he experiences from the possession of truth. He desires to be alone with God, and to hide from the profane world the graces he has received. Holy men do not talk about their holiness, **though it can clearly be seen from their deeds.**

Twelfth Week: Sunday.
The Pearl of Great Price.
St. Matt. xiii. 45, 46.

"Again, the Kingdom of Heaven is like to a merchant seeking good pearls, who when he had found one pearl of great price, went his way and sold all that he had, and bought it."

1. Every man in the world sets before himself some end to be attained in his actions. He is like a merchant collecting pearls. Around him lie scattered a number of such pearls, real or false. There is the pearl of money, the pearl of fame, the pearl of earthly love, the pearl of honour. Men buy these, and often buy them dear. But they are all worthless trash in comparison with the pearl of great price, the faithful performance day by day of the will of God, simply because it is His will.

2. This pearl often lies concealed in a rough and rugged shell. It is found under many an uncouth exterior, in the heart of many a one who is generally despised and held of no account. Beware then of despising any. The beggar in rags and filth may be a saint, and in his heart may be a pearl of virtue exceedingly beautiful in the eyes of God.

3. This pearl once recognized in its Divine beauty, the merchant cares little or nothing for the rest. He gladly barters them all for the one precious jewel which alone will shine in the Kingdom of God. Is this performance of the will of God the rule of my life? Do I value it and by its side despise all else?

Twelfth Week: Monday.
The Parable of the Leaven.
St. Matt. xiii. 33.

"The Kingdom of Heaven is like to leaven, which a woman took and hid in three measures of meal, until the whole was leavened."

1. Leaven is employed in Holy Scripture to express that which influences man, whether for good or for evil. St. Paul tells us to cast out the old leaven; the love of the world and of things sinful. Here our Lord speaks of the new leaven, the love of God and of things spiritual which has power to transform the soul. In my soul there is too much of the old leaven, too little of the new. O Christ, my Lord and Saviour, purge out the one and give me that love of Thee which alone can make me fitted for Thy company in Heaven.

2. What is the effect of leaven? It renders that which before was a heavy, hard, unwholesome lump, light and soft, and fit for the Master's table. So it is with the sweet influences of God's grace. The soul which before was sluggish and unable to rise to higher things, and unable to minister to the good of others, becomes active and zealous for God, light-hearted, and anxious to feed the souls of others with the bread of life.

3. The leaven leavens the whole mass in which it is placed, and extends to all the three measures. So the grace of God changes the whole soul; memory, intellect, and will, all are transformed. Words, acts, and thoughts, all feel the holy influence. Is my soul thus pervaded with this holy and Divine leaven?

Twelfth Week: Tuesday.
The Stilling of the Tempest.

St. Mark iv. 35—40.

When our Lord had finished His parables, He crossed the lake with His disciples, to avoid the multitudes. A great storm arose, and the boat was covered with waves, but Jesus was asleep in the stern. The Apostles awake Him and implore His aid, and He rebukes the wind and at once there is a great calm.

1. It was at the word of Jesus that the Apostles crossed the lake, and they looked for a prosperous voyage, but nevertheless a great storm arose and almost sunk their craft. So often, in the very work we have undertaken in obedience to the Divine command, a storm of troubles, and vexations, and disappointments arises. But, courage! the storm is only the prelude to some great happiness.

2. But not only was the voyage undertaken at His word, but He was with the disciples throughout it. Yet this did not hinder the rising of the storm. He was close at hand, apparently asleep and careless of their fate, but all the time watching to help them in the hour of need. So with His servants He is present, but His presence does not save them from sorrow, and suffering, and danger. He seems to be asleep but all the time He is but awaiting the moment when He may intervene with greater advantage to those whom He loves.

3. "Why are you fearful?" This was His word to the frightened Apostles. This is His word to us. Am not I master of the universe, and do not I love you fondly, tenderly, thoughtfully? I have but to say to the wind: "Peace, be still," and you will see a perfect calm and untroubled peace succeed the tempest that rages now.

Twel'th Week: Wednesday.
The Legion of Devils cast out.
St. Mark v. 1—20.

Jesus comes into the country of the Gerasenes, and there finds a man possess d by a legion of unclean spirits. The devils within him beseech our Lord not to torment them before the time. Jesus expels the unclean spirits, and gives them leave to occupy the bodies of a herd of swine feeding there, which straightway rush down the steep and perish in the sea.

1. This story shows the reality of demoniacal possession, and the awful power of the devils to torment their victim. Not one, but many—nay, a legion of devils occupied the body of this miserable man. Learn from this to dread the least yielding to the advances of Satan, and remember the ever-increasing power he gains over those who give him any advantage over them.

2. The devils, when they are cast out, beg not to be sent into the abyss, but to be allowed to enter the bodies of the swine feeding near. Nothing degrades like sin; the devils, in spite of the nobility of their angelic nature, find a congenial home in the swine. So it is with men who rebel against God and are lifted up with pride. God punishes them by handing them over to the indulgence of their lowest passions, and those who would fain be like God, become like the swine.

3. When the people of the place hear of the miracle wrought by our Lord, instead of falling at His feet in joy and gratitude, they beg Him to depart. They prefer to have the devils among them than Jesus, because His presence deprived them of their swine. Alas, how many choose the devil and his sensual attractions and worldly gains to the presence of Jesus!

Twelfth Week: Thursday.
The Old and the New.
St. Matt. ix. 14—17.

The disciples of John ask our Lord why His disciples do not fast. He answers that the friends of the bridegroom do not fast while the bridegroom is with them. God does not ask of men what is unsuitable to their circumstances or beyond their strength, just as men do not put a piece of raw cloth on an old garment, or new wine into old bottles.

1. The first reason that our Lord gives why His disciples do not observe special and voluntary fasts, is the fact of His presence. What room is there for penance when we are conscious that Jesus is with us, when we hear His voice speaking to our heart. The time will come when we shall mourn the loss of Him, when grace will seem to have departed from us, when sin will weigh heavily upon us, when we shall dread the Judgment. Then it is that He will call us to penance.

2. The second reason is, that as a piece of unfulled cloth patching an old garment only makes a greater rent, so if God asked too much of beginners, it would only destroy what is good in them. God gives only graces proportioned to our weakness. If we correspond to these, then we may afterwards hope for greater graces.

3. Lastly, men do not put new wine into skins that have hardened with age. So God does not give inspirations to high sanctity to those who are rooted in prejudice, or hardened by a worldly life. He gives them graces sufficient to save their souls, but nothing more at first. This it is which often excuses those whom we are prone to condemn.

Twelfth Week: Friday.
The Healing of the Woman with an Issue of Blood.
St. Mark v. 25—34.

A poor woman, who for twelve years had suffered from a continual loss of blood, and was continually becoming worse, comes in the crowd and touches the hem of Jesus' garment. She is instantly cured. Jesus asks who touched Him? The woman falls trembling at His feet, and is dismissed in peace.

1. Watch the scene. Our Lord, with the crowd pressing Him, and the disciples seeking to keep them away. How gentle He is! How kindly He welcomes all! What special love for the poor sinner! Observe the afflicted woman stealing up, trembling, but confident, and repeating to herself: "If I shall touch but His garment, I shall be healed." Admire her faith, and repeat her words, applying them to yourself.

2. Listen to what is spoken. Our Lord suddenly turns to His disciples, and asks, "Who touched Me?" The disciples wonder at the question. Were not the crowd thronging Him? Yet He knew the touch of one who came in faith and confidence and love. His Sacred Heart was drawn to her. When she comes up in fear lest she may have presumed, how kindly He receives her! So He always welcomes those who come near to His altar with dispositions like hers, humbly, yet boldly, half in fear, but with much love.

3. Notice the actions of those around. The poor woman is drawn to Jesus by His sweet attractions. Yet she must do her part if she is to be healed. Our Lord at first behaves as if He had not noticed her. Yet all the time He was thinking of her, blessing her, healing her, making her His own child.

Twelfth Week: Saturday.
The Raising of the Daughter of Jairus.
St. Mark v. 22—43.

Jairus, a ruler of the synagogue, has a little daughter at the point of death. Going to Jesus, he begs Him to come and lay His hand on her, that she may live. Jesus follows him, and on arrival at the house the child is dead, and the musicians, customary on such occasions, are assembled. Jesus puts them all out, and takes the maiden by the hand, and restores her to her parents.

1. This ruler of the synagogue was a wise man. He hastened to Jesus in his troubles, and told Him of the sorrow that threatened him, of the poor maiden in peril of death. Why do not we have recourse to Him, when those we love are in danger? Whether it be that their sickness is one of body or of soul, Jesus is always ready to listen, and will always come and comfort us in our distress.

2. Our Lord will not work the miracle until He has turned out the noisy and scoffing bystanders. His most wondrous works are done in silence and in retirement, and the babble of the noisy world seems to arrest His hand. It is in the peace and quiet of solitude and calm reflection, that the soul rises to new life : it must be alone with Jesus and shut out from worldly things, in order to hear His voice bidding it arise from the death of sin and the torpor of a careless life.

3. Her parents, in spite of their confidence in the power of Jesus, were astonished at seeing Him raise their child to life. We believe in Him in feeble fashion, but we do not at all appreciate His power and His love. If I did so more, I should obtain from Him blessings and graces altogether surpassing those granted me hitherto.

Thirteenth Week: Sunday.
The sending out of the Apostles to preach.
St. Matt. x. 1—10.

Our Lord, seeing the multitudes like sheep without a shepherd, calls the Apostles, and sends them out to preach and to heal the sick and cast out evil spirits and to raise the dead to life. They are to have no gold or silver, to be poorly clad, and to depend on the alms and hospitality of the faithful.

1. The occasion of the sending out of the Apostles was our Lord's pity for the sheep who had no shepherd, and who were lost because there was no one to invite them to penance. As it was then, so it is now. His Sacred Heart still mourns over the countless sheep who have no pastor. Alas! how many Catholics sit idle when they might help to bring back these wandering sheep. Do I do what I can for these shepherdless sheep by my own exertions, by alms, above all by prayers for them to the Good Shepherd?

2. Our Lord invests His Apostles with His own powers. All of them, even Judas, spoke with His authority. So now, each priest is invested with supernatural powers by Christ Himself, and claims respect, quite apart from his personal character. Do I show respect to every priest, and remember that I am to treat him as the special messenger of Jesus Christ?

3. These envoys of Christ are to beware of gold and silver. The love of money is fatal to all, most fatal to priests. They are to live a life of poverty and dependence, as every priest must do if he is to be an efficient servant of his Master; nay, as every ordinary Christian must do in his own degree, if he is to take part in the work of saving souls. Is this my spirit? or am I selfish and independent?

Thirteenth Week: Monday.
The Instructions for the Journey.
St. Matt. x. 11—17.

Our Lord instructs His Apostles that in every town they shall inquire who is a worthy man, and with him they shall lodge. They are to remain in his house until they leave the place. If any one refuses to receive them, or to listen to them the wrath of God will fall upon such a one for his rejection of the messengers of Christ. The servants of God must have the prudence of the serpent and the gentleness of the dove.

1. The Apostles on their journey are to lodge with some faithful servant of God, and our Lord promises that they will bring a blessing with them. To lodge and feed the ministers of God for their office' sake is a great privilege. since Christ has said, "He that receives you receives Me." In Catholic countries the visit of a priest is regarded as bringing a blessing on a house. Do you take every opportunity of showing hospitality to priests and other servants of God for their Master's sake?

2. The Apostles are not to move about from one house to another. Restlessness is always a bad sign. It is a common delusion to fancy that in another situation or house we shall do much better, and to believe that virtue will be easier elsewhere. It is a great grace to rest contented in the house and with the company in which God has placed us, and with the occupation He has given us.

3. The two virtues recommended by our Lord to His Apostles are extreme gentleness and continual prudence. Without gentleness we shall never win souls to Christ. Every good man is gentle. Without prudence we shall spoil our work by acting foolishly and rashly. Both of these are supernatural gifts, which cannot be had without prayer and self-conquest.

Thirteenth Week: Tuesday.
Our Lord's care of His Servants.
St. Matt. x. 26—33.

The servants of Christ have no cause to fear even in the midst of their most bitter enemies. Not a hair of their head falls to the ground without God's permission. He who cares for each sparrow, cares for them. Those who confess Him, He will confess at the Judgment before all the world.

1. It requires no little courage to go forth in the character of sheep amid wolves hungry for their prey. So to face persecution is no easy task. But He who made Stephen joyful when stoned, and Laurence when roasted on the gridiron, is present to each one who suffers for Him, and pours into the heart of the sufferer peace and joy. If He watches over every sparrow, how much more over every one of His servants. O Lord, give me courage in the day of trial, and help to persevere amid suffering.

2. Christ will reward with a most liberal recompense the loyalty of all His faithful servants who stand up for Him in the face of opposition. Some have to face death for Christ; others cruel suffering. Some have to submit to ridicule, others to unkind treatment. All have sometimes to withstand the influence and example of those around, and bravely to refuse to take part in evil; it may be in uncharitable or unseemly conversation, or in disrespectful words of those set over them. On such occasions do I confess Christ?

3. Those who refuse to confess Christ deny Him; not in so many words, but in joining in what they know is hateful to Him they virtually deny Him, and refuse to acknowledge His authority. Alas! I have often done this. I have been ashamed of **Thee, I have denied Thee. Jesus, forgive me, and do not disown me before the Angels of God**

Thirteenth Week: Wednesday.
The Warfare of the Gospel.
St. Matt. x. 34—39.

Christ comes not to send peace on earth, but a sword, to set men at variance with those nearest and dearest to them. Above all else, Him we must love; Him we must follow, bearing our cross; of Him we are not worthy unless we are willing to suffer for His sake.

1. It seems strange that the Prince of Peace should come to send a sword upon earth. Yet He knew that true peace cannot be had without war, and that in many a house by reason of Him there would arise a bitter strife, and those who love Him would have to suffer persecution of some kind at the hands of those dear to them. I must be prepared for this; I must expect and bear patiently for love of Him disagreeables at the hand of others.

2. When there comes a contest between earthly affection and the love of Christ, God grant that earthly affection may not prevail. How many have lost their souls for the sake of some one to whom their heart goes out with fond desire! If that time comes to me, I must be brave. I must remember that if I sacrifice Christ, even for one dear to me as my life, I shall lose my soul, and perhaps, too, the soul of the object of my love. If I make the sacrifice, then and then only I shall have peace here and hereafter.

3. In this, and in many other ways, I must carry my cross willingly, not reluctantly; out of love for Jesus, not because I cannot get rid of it. It is a heavy one perhaps, but prayer and submission, and the thought of Him who carried His Cross for me, will lighten it. And in the end, the heavier **the cross, the brighter the crown.**

Thirteenth Week: Thursday.
The Recompense of Charity.
St. Matt. x. 40—42.

If we receive one of the servants of Christ in His Name, we shall receive the same recompense as if we received Christ Himself, and we share the reward that the prophet or just man shall himself receive. Even a cup of cold water given to one of the least of Christ's disciples, because he is a disciple of Christ, will not lose its reward.

1. "He that receiveth you receiveth Me." This is not true of the Apostles alone, but of all to whom we show charity for Christ's sake; those who tend the sick in the hospitals for love of Christ, are really tending Christ Himself; those who visit the widows and fatherless in their affliction are really visiting Christ Himself; those who give alms to the poor from a supernatural motive are really putting the money into the hand of Christ Himself.

2. When we treat with charity any of the delegates of Christ, we identify ourselves with the work they do, and earn a share in the special reward they will receive. One who receives and lodges missionaries and aids in their work, or lay-brothers and lay-sisters sent round to beg, will have a part in their reward. This extends to any good work that we aid with alms or prayers or any other encouragement for Christ's sake.

3. More than this, every little kindness however minute, done, not from mere natural benevolence or affection, but explicitly and implicitly for the love of Christ, will have a reward to all eternity. How eagerly should I embrace all such occasions, and how careful should I be in every such act, to offer it to God, and so obtain the supernatural **reward.**

Thirteenth Week: Friday.
The Death of St. John the Baptist.
St. Mark vi. 17—29.

When Herod heard of the miracles of Jesus, he thought that St. John the Baptist had risen from the dead. Herod had imprisoned John because he reproved him for taking his brother's wife. But he feared John, and did many things at his advice. At length at a banquet, rashly promising to the daughter of Herodias anything she asked, he was persuaded by her against his will to order the beheading of John.

1. Herod's guilty conscience suspected the reappearance of the holy man he had put to death. He knew that the ill-deeds we do sleep but are not dead. When I look back on my past life, is there any sin that I specially dread, or any one who will rise up as my accuser and charge me with wrong done to him !

2. Herod respected and liked St. John. He listened to him with pleasure. He often did good deeds, and abstained from sin at his instance. But he would not give up his cherished sin; he would not put away Herodias. So in my heart is there any sin to which I cling? Any Herodias whom I will not put away? Any cherished fault that spoils my life before God?

3. How little Herod thought when he sat down to that royal banquet, and ordered in the dancing girl to amuse his guests, that before that night he would have sealed his guilt by the cruel murder of one of the Saints of God ! Notice the steps that led to his final guilt : (1) unlawful affection indulged ; (2) persecution of the Saint who reproved him ; (3) the neglect of warnings ; (4) sensual indulgence ; (5) the rash oath ; and then at length **the murder of one of the Saints of God.**

Thirteenth Week: Saturday.
The Return of the Apostles.
St. Mark vi. 30—35.

The Apostles returning, relate to their Master all that they have done and taught. He invites them to come to some quiet place and rest awhile. But soon the multitudes find them out, and flock to Jesus from all the towns and villages of the country round.

1. The Apostles give to Jesus a full account of their mission, and of all that they have done and taught. Each evening when I examine my conscience I ought to tell Him in like manner all that I can remember of the day. He is interested in every detail. I will tell Him my troubles of the day; the faults committed, the efforts I have made to please Him, the work that I have done for Him; and I will offer Him all that is good, and ask Him to forgive the many defects, to accept my works and words to promote His glory.

2. After their labours, Jesus proposes to His Apostles an interval of repose. He is a thoughtful and good Master, Who never forgets the wants of His servants. Sometimes I fancy He has forgotten me, but it is not so. If I wait a little, I shall find that He was merely devising some fresh way of promoting my happiness and my welfare.

3. The multitudes will not give our Lord any rest. Vainly He resorts to a desert-place. They soon find Him out there. Yet could He not have checked them by a word or a thought, and prevented their intrusion upon His solitude? Why did He not do so? Because it was the will of His Heavenly Father that He should suffer all the inconveniences as well as the sorrows of human life, so that no incident of whatever kind may be unknown to Him.

Fourteenth Week: Sunday.
The Feeding of the Five Thousand.
St. Matt. xiv. 14—22.

The multitudes who had followed Jesus found themselves at the close of day destitute of all food for their support. He will not send them away, but orders them to sit down on the grass, and then taking five loaves and two fishes which one of His disciples had brought, He blesses them, and by His blessing multiplies them, so tnat all those who are present eat and are filled.

1. The importunate crowd, which had followed Jesus to the desert-place when He had sought to be alone with His Apostles, received from Him the kindest welcome. No angry word at their intrusion; no abrupt dismissal; nothing but gentleness and kindness and sympathy and love. How differently we treat those who interrupt us and disturb us untimely, and thrust themselves upon us when we desire to be alone.

2. Our Lord's charity to the multitude did not end with words. His compassion was an effective compassion. It brought solid relief. It was a universal compassion extending to body as well as to soul. It was a prompt compassion, taking action at once to provide for the needs of the multitude. I am sometimes moved to pity: does my compassion resemble His in these particulars?

3. This miracle was a type of the Blessed Eucharist. It was a preparation for it. If Christ could multiply the loaves and fishes so that each could partake of them, why should He not so multiply His Sacred Body and Blood that all the faithful who approach the altar should receive Christ Himself in all His Divine perfections? Learn from this miracle a strong faith in His Presence in each Sacred Host.

Fourteenth Week: Monday.
The Gathering up of the Fragments.
St. John vi. 12, 13.

When the multitude had eaten and were satisfied, Jesus commands His disciples to go round and gather up the fragments that remained, and they gathered twelve full baskets.

1. Let us contemplate the scene. The Apostles first carrying round among the people the basket containing the five loaves and two fishes, and always finding enough and more than enough for each of the companies into which the crowd was broken up. The hungry crowd eating this miraculous banquet in wondering gratitude and awe. Jesus moving to and fro among them, looking to the wants of all, with a kind and cheering word for each, making all happy with His Divine presence. So now, in Holy Communion, when His priests distribute the Bread of Heaven, He desires to see all happy, and has for each a holy inspiration and a word of comfort.

2. When our Lord provides for His servants, He does not provide sparingly. He is generous and bountiful, and gives good measure and running over. He gave the crowd not merely just enough to keep them from starving, but as much as they could eat and more. So He has been and is very generous to me, and will be more generous still if I am generous with Him.

3. Jesus will not allow the natural law of frugality and poverty to be neglected because, forsooth, He can by a word provide for all the wants of His people. No fragment of the broken food is to be wasted. The possession of plenty is no excuse for wastefulness. There is a special blessing on careful attention to little things, and those who are most truly generous are often those who are most careful not to spend a penny thoughtlessly.

Fourteenth Week: Tuesday.
Jesus appears walking upon the Lake.
St. Matt. xiv. 22—33.

After the multitude was dismissed, our Lord went up into a mountain to pray. Meanwhile, the disciples were crossing the lake to Bethsaida. Wind and waves were against them, and they laboured in rowing. Suddenly, Jesus is seen by them walking upon the water. They cry out in fear, but Jesus consoles them: "It is I, fear not."

1. The disciples embarked at Jesus' command, full of awe, and wonder, and confidence at the miracle just wrought. Their voyage was a stormy and perilous one. Why did their all-powerful Master leave them in such straits? So now, God gives us some signal grace, and soon after we have to struggle against circumstances the most adverse. Everything seems against us. Has our Master deserted and forgotten us?

2. No, He has not forgotten His faithful servants, and soon amid their struggles they see One walking on the sea. Yet they do not recognize Him; in their terror they fancy that it is some apparition boding ill to them, perhaps a messenger of destruction. So too, when we are down-hearted and in difficulties, we shrink in terror from the very source of consolation. Jesus comes to us under the form of one who is destined to deliver us, and we shrink from Him, or regard the hand that would deliver us as the hand of a foe.

3. But their compassionate Master will not leave them long in their dismay. With consoling words He speaks to their hearts. "Be of good heart, it is I, be not afraid." So too, if I listen in my troubles, I shall hear the same loving voice echoing in my ears. Jesus is near at hand, though I know it **not**.

Fourteenth Week: Wednesday.
St. Peter walks upon the Water.
St. Matt. xiv. 28—31.

When Jesus speaks, Peter makes answer: "Lord if it be Thou, bid me come to Thee upon the waters." Jesus bids him come, and he walks upon the waves, until, beginning to fear, he begins to sink, and cries: "Lord, save me." Jesus stretches out His hand and takes him, and says: "O thou of little faith, wherefore didst thou doubt?"

1. St. Peter recognized His Master's voice, and asked that he might be allowed to tread the angry waves to come to Him. Here observe (1) St. Peter's ready faith at Jesus' words. (2) His boldness in action, a boldness, moreover, which was not presumptuous, for (3) he waited for Jesus' bidding to come. (4) His desire to be at Jesus' side during the raging storm. Learn from each of these a lesson for yourself.

2. But though Peter had not over-estimated the power of His Master, he had over-estimated his own courage. When the wind swept fiercely by, and the waters surged around, he began to be afraid, and straightway began to sink. So now, how many a failure is due to want of courage. We lose heart; we forget God's power and think of our own weakness, and we thus bring upon ourselves the very failures that we dread. How many a sin, too, comes of want of courage. I lost heart; I got discouraged; I thought it was no use trying; so I fell.

3. When he begins to sink, Peter, like a good and wise man, turns to his Master: "Lord, save me." Jesus at once stretches out His hand, and Peter fears no longer, sinks no more. When our courage fails, this must be our cry: Lord, save me! of myself I cannot but sink, but stretch out Thy hand, and I am safe!

Fourteenth Week: Thursday.
The Meat that perisheth.
St. John vi. 25—27.

The crowds find Jesus on the other side of the lake, and are reproached by Him with seeking Him for the sake of the loaves and fishes, not because of the miracles that He wrought. He urges them to labour for the meat that endures to life everlasting, which the Son of Man would give them.

1. What does our Lord mean by His reproof to the multitude? Was it not because of His miracles that they sought Him? It was for the sake of the temporal benefits, not for His own sake. We must not allow ourselves to lose sight of Jesus in the wonders He performs for us. There is such a thing as an interested following of Him because of the pleasure we derive from His service. This will not please Him: it must be for His own sake that we seek Him. We must cling to Him amid darkness and suffering.

2. "Labour not for the meat that perisheth." How necessary is this warning for all! Our end in life is too often not the greater glory of God, but our own honour, comfort, pleasure, riches. Insensibly God fades out of sight, and too often, when there are conflicting interests, the interests of God are sacrificed. We accept the meat that perishes, the enjoyment of the hour, perhaps the sinful and inordinate enjoyment, and wilfully and deliberatively neglect the will of God.

3. If we knew the delicious sweetness of the meat that endures to everlasting life, how eagerly should we seek after it! How distasteful, how unattractive would all else appear! O my God, grant me the happiness of knowing and tasting the sweetness of that meat which Jesus and Jesus alone can give.

Fourteenth Week: Friday.
The Bread from Heaven.
St. John vi. 29—35.

The Jews further ask our Lord for some sign like that of the manna. Jesus answers that His Father in Heaven will give them at once sign and substance, the true Bread from Heaven; that He was that true Bread which would satisfy their hunger and quench their thirst, so that they would never hunger or thirst again.

1. The question of the Jews did not imply any doubt as to the miracle of the loaves and fishes, but they desired a proof that Jesus had the power and the will, not once only, but always, to supply their needs, as the manna supplied them day by day. This is the real test of every good influence, whether it will last and produce permanent, not temporary effects. Do my good resolutions and promises thus stand the test of time?

2. Our Lord answers that His Father in Heaven will give them a bread that will impart fresh life to the world; a spiritual, supersubstantial bread, that comes down from Heaven, the Bread of God, that will satisfy every desire of the heart, and fill the soul with joy and peace. Feed my soul, O God, with that Bread, and may it ever nourish in me the love of Thee and likeness to Thee.

3. When the Jews cry out, "Lord, give us always this Bread," Jesus answers that He is this Bread of Life, that those who go nigh to Him should have a bread that would cause them never again to hunger, and streams of the water of life that would quench their thirst for ever. O Jesus, grant that receiving Thee, I may be thus satisfied, and that all earthly desires may be swallowed up in my desire after Thee!

Fourteenth Week: Saturday.
The Saving Will of God.
St. John vi. 36—40.

Jesus goes on to tell the Jews that He will cast out none who come to Him in faith, and that such are given to Him by His Father, because He came down from Heaven to do the will of His Father, not His own; that all such who believe on Him will have life everlasting, and He will raise them up to eternal life.

1. "Him that cometh to Me I will not cast out." These are the words of consolation that have saved many a poor sinner from despair. The all-embracing love of Jesus! This it is that brings Heaven so near to us all. He yearns over every sinner, and the more deeply-dyed his sin, the greater the compassion of the Divine Saviour. If he will but come and throw himse'f at His feet, He is ready, He is longing, to forgive all. "Him that cometh unto Me I will no wise cast out."

2. All who come in this spirit are given to Jesus by His Eternal Father. They are His own, marked by His seal unto eternal life; and even though they may wander for a time, yet He will bring them back, and casting themselves at His feet, they will be forgiven. As long as they do not give up their confidence in Him, He will not let them perish, but will bring them safe to everlasting life.

3. Jesus earned this gift from His Eternal Father by His renunciation of His own will while on earth. This is the secret of helping others, of influencing others. The self-willed never have any influence with God; somehow He heeds them not. It is they who joyfully give up what they themselves desire for God's sake, who obtain from Him **all they desire.**

Fifteenth Week: Sunday.
The Murmuring of the Jews.
St. John vi. 41—52.

The Jews are angry when Jesus tells them that He is the Living Bread that came down from Heaven. They declare that He is of human parentage. Then He repeats His words, and tells them still more explicitly in what sense He is the Bread from Heaven. "The Bread that I will give is My Flesh for the life of the world."

1. To the minds of the Jews there was present on the one hand the general belief that Jesus was the Son of Joseph, and on the other His own assertion that He came down from Heaven. Were they to credit the word of Christ or not? This depended on their good-will. So now, belief in miracles, in the Church, in all that God reveals, depends on the disposition of the heart. Am I so obedient to the voice of God within me as to deserve the clearness of mental vision granted to the obedient?

2. Jesus does not tone down His assertions in order to meet half-way the views of doubters, but rather puts more clearly the unpalatable truths which they refuse to accept. It is no use thinking to win over sceptics or non-Catholics by a sort of liberalism and by watering down Divine truth. We must be careful not to exaggerate, but we must be careful not to detract from truth to please those who do not believe.

3. Hitherto the Divine Teacher had veiled under parables that central doctrine of the Blessed Eucharist which the miracle of the feeding of the five thousand had prefigured, but now He speaks plainly, "The Bread that I will give is My Flesh." Grant to me, O Lord, to have ever a firm faith in this inscrutable and Divine Mystery.

Fifteenth Week: Monday.
The Question of Unbelief.

St. John vi. 53.

When the Jews heard our Lord declare plainly that the Bread that He would give was His own Flesh, they asked incredulously: "How can this Man give us His Flesh to eat?"

1. This question is one which has been asked by heretics from the beginning of the world till now. They have one and all denied the change of the substance in the Blessed Sacrament. They have asked the question of the Jews, and answered, Impossible! But that which is impossible with men is possible with God; and the miracle of the Blessed Eucharist is the object of the steadfast faith of every Catholic throughout the world. Thank God for the faith He has given you, and do not forget to pray for those who deny and blaspheme this sacred truth.

2. Some there are who do not deny the presence of the Body and Blood of Christ in some fashion, but answer that Christ gives us His Body and Blood by faith. Others that He does so figuratively, inasmuch as He nourishes our souls. Others that He is really present, but that the change of the substance is a fiction of theologians. Try and realize that the Body of Christ that hung upon the Cross is really present in the Sacred Host, and that the same Blood that was shed for you is received by you in Holy Communion, and adored upon the altar.

3. Why did Jesus make this eating of His Flesh a condition of life? To show us how He still loves to humble Himself; to teach us the closeness of the union that He desires between Himself and us; to give us a healing remedy against every sickness of the soul. O love unspeakable!

Fifteenth Week: Tuesday.
Backsliding Disciples.
St. John vi. 61—72.

Many of the disciples of our Lord refuse to accept His teaching respecting the Blessed Eucharist, and fall away from Him. When He appeals to the Twelve, "Will you also go away?" Peter with generous loyalty exclaims: "Lord, to whom shall we go? Thou hast the words of eternal life."

1. The doctrines of revelation not only enable the true and faithful friends of Jesus to draw more closely to Him, but they also sift out the wheat from the chaff, the men of good-will from those whose pride will not submit absolutely to the Divine Teacher. In the commands of the Gospel, by His holy inspiration, or the voice of our superiors, Christ sometimes asks hard things of us. Then it is that our loyalty is tested, and it is seen whether humility or obedience is the guiding principle of our life. How do I behave under such circumstances?

2. The Heart of Jesus is pierced with sorrow at this infidelity of the children dear to Him. There is something plaintive in His appeal to the Twelve, "Will you also go away?" We little know how we wound that Sacred Heart when we refuse to obey, or when we are self-willed and unfaithful to His heavenly guidance.

3. Listen to Peter's faithful words of love, "Lord, to whom shall we go? Thou hast the words of eternal life." It was this loyalty that made him so dear to Jesus. Repeat his words. Lord, to whom shou'd I go but to Thee in all my difficulties, trials, temptations? Thou hast the words that are music in my ears; the words which are an echo of Heaven's melodies. In Thee I live; **Thee alone I love**; may I ever be faithful to **Thee!**

Fifteenth Week: Wednesday.
The Unwashed Hands.
St. Mark vii. 1—9.

The Pharisees complain to Jesus that His disciples do not observe the accustomed ceremonial of washing before every meal. Jesus reproves them as hypocrites, and as teaching the precepts of men in the place of the commandments of God.

1. What was it that so displeased our Lord in these observances of the Pharisees? It was not the mere fact of washing nor the holding to ancient traditions, but the substitution of external forms for obedience to the precepts of God. This sort of hypocrisy is hateful to God. Instead of observing God's law they violated it deliberately, and in their pride thought that they would be justified by the superior sanctity involved in practising a certain ritual which was but of human authority. Beware of formalism and of thinking yourself a person of superior virtue because you are more exact in religious observances than others.

2. The Pharisees also clung to these ceremonies on account of their pride, which made them regard it as a stain on their nobility to be brought into contact with other men. They, therefore, must wash themselves clean before they could even take a meal. Anything that implies contempt of others is very displeasing to God, just as honour shown to them for His sake receives a liberal reward.

3. To honour God with our lips while our hearts are far away is hateful to God. This does not mean that involuntary distractions in our prayers are a sin, but that to pretend to obey Him while we are really in rebellion against Him is most displeasing to Him. So also is the deliberate giving of our thoughts to worldly subjects during the times of prayer or Holy Mass.

Fifteenth Week : Thursday.
The Growth of Corrupt Traditions.

St. Mark vii. 10—13.

Our Lord reproves the Jews for breaking through the Law of God in order to keep their own traditions, and especially for allowing a son to neglect his duty to his parents on the ground that he has given to God what he ought to have contributed to their support.

1. Our duty to God can never set aside our duty to other men. The former, except in cases where He Himself directly interposes, is never at variance with any strict obligation of the natural law. He who is bound to maintain his aged father or mother cannot evade this duty on the ground that he has given to God what is due to them. Under pretence of honouring God, the evil custom of the Jews set aside the sacred duty of a son to honour his parents. Is this duty to father, mother, those about you, one which you observe with loyalty?

2. Our Lord's words teach us how careful we must be not to mistake self-will and selfish aims for loyalty to God. Those who neglect home duties for works outside or for practices of piety, or to frequent the services of the Church, are like those whom Christ here condemns. If ever there is a question between presence at Holy Mass and attendance by a sick bed, do not forget that charity should carry the day.

3. We must at the same time bear in mind that when God calls us we must be ready to leave home and friends and parents, when we hear His voice. Parental authority ceases before the superior claim of the Most High. But we must be very sure that He is calling us, and must follow the advice of some prudent counsellor and not our own in our decision.

Fifteenth Week: Friday.
Evil Thoughts.
St. Mark vii. 21—23.

"Out of the heart of men proceed evil thoughts, adulteries, fornications, murders, thefts, covetousness, wickedness, deceit, lasciviousness, an evil eye, blasphemy, pride, foolishness; all these evil things come from within and defile a man."

1. There are very few who are not sometimes tempted to evil thoughts. They crowd into the mind at all times and places, they are present before we are conscious of them; they often refuse to depart, and if for a short time they are absent, they recur again more vividly than ever. We cannot flee from them. O God! in Thy mercy preserve me from evil thoughts.

2. What do we mean by evil thoughts? We mean the presence of some imagination in which it is sinful to take pleasure, or the forming of an intention the fulfilment of which would be a sin of act. Such is the list given by our Lord. They fall under two main heads: thoughts against charity, thoughts against purity. But there are many beside, thoughts of pride, thoughts of vanity, thoughts of covetousness, &c. To which class am I most prone? And do I resist them?

3. What is the source of evil thoughts? Sometimes they arise from and are a punishment for past sins. Sometimes they come of present carelessness, or from neglect in the custody of our senses. Sometimes they arise from the frailty of human nature; sometimes from the malice of the devil. Are they always sinful? We shall see in our next meditation,

Fifteenth Week: Saturday.
The Sinfulness of Evil Thoughts.

St. Mark vii. 21—23.

"Out of the heart of men proceed evil thoughts. ... These evil things come from within and defile a man."

1. Are evil thoughts always sinful? Certainly not. Their mere presence is no sin at all. They are only sinful when we wilfully consent to them. If this consent is a partial and momentary consent, they amount to a venial sin; but if it is a full and deliberate consent to that which in act would be a mortal sin, then a mortal sin of thought is committed. If there is included in the thought a desire to commit the sin if opportunity offer, the sin is thereby aggravated; as if we should not only indulge thoughts of deadly hatred, but should also resolve to injure seriously the person hated. Do I ever indulge such sins of thought?

2. Most of us are in continual danger of at least venial sins, in the shape of unkind thoughts towards those who we think have offended us, and to this perhaps we add a desire of some petty revenge. Some too are constantly tempted to indulge some sort of imaginations contrary to the angelical virtue. Sometimes, too, human affection or passion leads us to let our thoughts dwell on dangerous objects. O my God! grant that my heart may be so united to Thee in charity that I may turn away my mind from thoughts displeasing to Thee.

3. We need not be discouraged by evil thoughts if we do our best to be rid of them. They may haunt us continually, they may refuse to depart; yet as long as we do not yield, but hate them and try to resist them, we need not fear. Nay, we are earning merit in God's sight by fighting against these enemies that assail us in spite of ourselves,

Sixteenth Week: Sunday.
The Syrophœnician Woman.
St. Mark vii. 24—30.

When Jesus was in the extreme north of Palestine, a Gentile woman came, and falling down before Him, entreated Him to heal her daughter who was possessed by a devil. Jesus answered her that it was not good to take the children's bread and cast it to the dogs. The woman, nothing disconcerted, urged that the whelps also eat of the crumbs from the master's table. Our Lord, touched by her humility, heals her child.

1. The petition of this poor heathen woman did not appear at first to be favourably received by Jesus. His answer to her was a decided rebuff. It is not good to take the food that belongs to the children of God and give it to the dogs outside the fold. So our Lord often seems to receive our petitions in a way not at all flattering to ourselves, and to reject us in favour of the privileged Jews who are preferred to us. Yet He all the time is only wounding that He may afterwards heal.

2. Observe the humility of this poor woman. Instead of resenting the rebuff she had received and the apparent partiality of Jesus, she admits that she is but a dog, unworthy of the children's bread, but to whom perhaps some broken meat may out of generosity be given. Do I take well rebuff and speeches which wound self-love? There is no better test of holiness than this.

3. Humility, as usual, brings its own reward. "The prayer of the humble pierceth the clouds." God can refuse nothing to those who are truly humble. Humble yourselves, then, before God, acknowledge your own vileness, then you may hope for great things from Him.

Sixteenth Week: Monday.
The Deaf and Dumb Man healed.
St. Mark vii. 31—37.

Near the Sea of Galilee there is brought to Jesus one deaf and dumb. Jesus takes him apart, puts His fingers in his ears and touches His tongue with His sacred spittle ; and looking up to Heaven, says, "Ephpheta, be thou opened." At once his ears are opened and he hears aright.

1. Deafness and dumbness in the things of God generally go together. If we do not listen to God's voice speaking to us, we shall not speak aright on subjects connected with God. Every great theologian joins prayer to study : all really successful preachers have sought the help of God, and have prayed Him to put words in their mouths. He who listens not to God may utter words, but not words which will reach the hearing of those who listen.

2. Why does Jesus, who might have cured the deaf and dumb man with a word, put His fingers in his ears and touch his tongue with His spittle? To teach us the importance of ceremonies, and of using rites and forms as a means of impressing Divine truths on those who receive and who witness them. Learn to value the ceremonies of the Church, each of which has its own lesson to convey, and its own meaning sanctioned by God Himself.

3. The Church preserves the memory of this miracle in Holy Baptism. The priest touches with his spittle the ears and mouth of the infant, using our Lord's own word : "Ephpheta." That signifies that until Jesus opens the ears to hear the words of God, and the lips to speak Divine truths, they are deaf to His voice, and dumb to speak His praises. It is He who must open our ears, enlighten **our hearts, and put good words into our mouth.**

Sixteenth Week: Tuesday.
The Sign from Heaven.
St. Matt. xvi. 1—4.

When the Pharisees asked for a sign from Heaven, Jesus gave them in answer the red sky at evening as promising fine weather, at morning as foretelling a storm. He then reproves them for their hypocrisy in that they ignore the signs from which they might have learnt the coming of the Kingdom of God, though they are quick enough to discern the signs of the times.

1. To seek for a supernatural sign as a condition of belief is a common excuse for scepticism and indifference. Men want to make their own terms with God. They will believe on Him if He will do this or that. Thus to dictate to Him is a presumption which He will not brook; or at most it is a superstition that He will certainly disregard. We cannot discover His will by tokens that we choose at our own will.

2. In the same way we cannot find out what is the best course for us to pursue by these arbitrary and self-chosen means. God has provided means, and these, these alone, will guide us aright. He has laid down practical rules for us. He tells us to wait and reflect and pray, and to be on our guard against natural impulses, to commit our difficulties to Him. Do I use these means when I am in doubt?

3. The sin of the Pharisees consisted in their wilful blindness to the signs God Himself had provided. "If you believe not Me," says our Lord, "believe the works." The sin consisted in the rejection of these proofs of His Divinity. This is the sin of moderns who turn away from the Church. She has the marks of her divinity upon her, but men will not accept her teaching and submit to her guidance.

Sixteenth Week: Wednesday.
The Leaven of the Pharisees.
St. Matt. xvi. 5—12.

As the disciples are crossing the Sea of Galilee with our Lord, He warns them against the leaven of the Pharisees. It happened that they had forgotten to bring any bread with them, and they thought that He referred to this. He reproved them for the want of confidence in His power that was implied in their supposition that He was warning them against the bread of the Pharisees, and explained to them that it was the false teaching and hypocrisy of the Pharisees that He wished to avoid.

1. The leaven of any set of men is that which leavens the body at large; the leaven of a man's life is that which leavens and influences all his actions. The leaven of the Pharisees was their doctrine; not that it was all bad, but the prevailing element that affected it all was corrupt and opposed to the precepts of the Gospel. So we see in the doctrine of those who depart from the Church's teaching much that is good, but it is leavened by the underlying rottenness of their position.

2. So a set of men may do works externally good and may appear of unspotted and holy life. Yet if pride underlies it all, if their hearts are set on themselves and not on God, then this leaven affects it and infects all they do. All is rotten in God's sight and offensive to Him. Alas! is not my life infected by such leaven of pride?

3. Such men our Lord called *hypocrites, i.e.*, they are actors, playing a part and using words which are at variance with the motives of their actions. They may not detect these, but God sees through the outwardly fair-seeming action and pierces to its centre. Can I stand this test? What is the aspect **of my actions to His all-seeing eye?**

Sixteenth Week: Thursday.
The Blind Man at Bethsaida.
St. Mark. viii. 22—26.

At Bethsaida a blind man is brought to our Lord, with a request that He would touch his eyes. Jesus leads him out of the town, and laying His hands on his eyes, asks him whether he sees anything. The man answers: "I see men as trees walking." Again He touches his eyes, and this time he sees clearly.

1. The blind man brought to our Lord is a type of those who cannot see their way in spiritual things. They have some fault, but they do not see how to cure it; some aspiration after a higher life, and they do not see how to carry it out; some desire to labour for others, and these seem insuperable hindrances in their way. In such circumstances we must have recourse to Jesus, and ask Him to lead us in our blindness and to give us sight that we may know whither to turn our steps.

2. The blind man did not recover his sight all at once, even under the healing hand of the Good Physician. This was because he had not sufficient faith and confidence in Jesus. His dispositions were still imperfect, and therefore he was only capable at first of a partial cure. So is it often with us. The real reason for our sight being so dim and for our inability to see our way clearly is because our good-will is not firm; we are not completely detached from the faults and sins that obscure our vision.

3. A second time Jesus lays His hand on him, and now he sees clearly. We must not expect one Communion or Novena to obtain all that we ask. We must ask our Lord to return to us, to complete His good work in us, and He will not fail to listen in the end.

Sixteenth Week: Friday.
The Confession of St. Peter.

St. Matt. xvi. 13—16.

When Jesus asked His disciples, "Whom do you say that I am?" Peter answered, "Thou art the Christ, the Son of the living God." Jesus answering, said to him, "Blessed art thou, Simon Bar-jona, because flesh and blood hath not revealed it to thee, but My Father who is in Heaven."

1. The question that Jesus asked of His Apostles was not asked for His own sake, but for theirs. It was a test of their loyalty, that they might have the privilege of proclaiming His Divinity. The angels and saints in Heaven consider it an honour to proclaim the glory of the Son of God: how much more is it man's highest honour to bear witness to the Divinity of Jesus What a privilege we should think it to sing His praises, to proclaim our faith in Him, and above all, to adore Him in the Blessed Sacrament of the Altar.

2. Peter calls Christ the Son of the living God to show that He was His Son by nature, not by adoption; that He was Very God of Very God, and not the Son of God merely as the Prophets were also the sons of God. It is this which gives to Jesus all power in Heaven and earth. He, our Brother, Friend, the sweet Lover of our souls, is nevertheless the Omnipotent God. How happy we are to have such a Friend! Why do we not make better use of His Divine Friendship?

3. Jesus proclaims Peter blessed because, under the inspiration of God, he had proclaimed that mystery of mysteries, the Incarnation of the Eternal Word. Thank God that to you also God has revealed this mystery, that you enjoy the inestimable blessings of the Catholic faith.

Sixteenth Week: Saturday.
The Promise to St. Peter.

St. Matt. xvi. 17—19.

"Thou art Peter; and upon this rock I will build My Church, and the gates of Hell shall not prevail against it. And I will give to thee the keys of the Kingdom of Heaven. And whatever thou shalt bind on earth, it shall be bound also in Heaven: and whatsoever thou shalt loose on earth, it shall be loosed also in Heaven."

1. Our Lord in these words gives the Catholic Church its charter and its earthly sovereignty. It is to be built on the rock of Peter, and Peter's successors are to rule it to the very end of time. This is what no heretic will allow, even although he allow all else. This is the touchstone of the true Catholic, viz., loyalty to the Holy See; a readiness to accept all that comes from Rome, and to obey every command and every wish that proceeds from the mouth of the Vicar of Christ.

2. Against the Church founded on Peter the gates of Hell shall never prevail. It is strange that those outside the Church do not recognize in her indefectibility the mark of her Divine mission. The tempest-tossed bark of Peter has continually seemed to be on the point of being submerged, when suddenly it has appeared unharmed and triumphant, riding over the billows that threatened its destruction. Thank God for this wondrous gift, and for your being safe in Peter's bark.

3. To Peter and his successors are given the keys of the Kingdom of Heaven. They are therefore endowed with authority over the House of which Christ is the Lord. What reverence is consequently due to the Holy Father, and to all bishops and priests, who in their various degrees share his authority, and bear the commission of Christ Himself!

Seventeenth Week: Sunday.
The Approaching Passion.
St. Matt. xvi. 21—23.

During the earlier portion of His Ministry our Lord had but darkly hinted at His coming Passion and Death. But now He begins to teach them that He must suffer many things from the ancients and the Chief Priests, and be put to death, and the third day rise again. Peter remonstrates: "Lord, this shall not be." But Jesus reproves him and says: "Get thee behind Me, Satan."

1. Our Lord does not teach the doctrine of the Cross at once to His Apostles, lest it should be too hard for them. He waits until they are thoroughly convinced under the guidance of the Holy Spirit that He is the Son of God. So we must be very careful how we thrust upon those who are imperfectly instructed or full of prejudice the more difficult dogmas of the Faith, or we may repel where we might have attracted.

2. It must have been a relief to our Blessed Lord's human desire after sympathy to communicate to His Apostles the sufferings He was to undergo. It is always a relief to human nature to tell to those we love our fears and anxieties, our sorrows and our joys. Do I try to throw myself into the troubles of others, and lay myself out to try and lighten their sufferings by my sympathy and ready compassion?

3. In St. Peter's kindly expostulation was involved a temptation from the Evil One to turn away from the chalice of suffering. Because Jesus shrank from the coming agony, He turns the more indignantly on the tempter who would dissuade Him from it. When I have to face suffering, am I thus **loyal to God?**

Seventeenth Week: Monday.
The Doctrine of the Cross.
St. Mark viii. 34—38.

Our Lord proclaims to His disciples that whoever will come after Him must deny himself and take up his cross and follow Him; whoever seeks to save his life at the expense of loyalty to Christ shall lose it, and whoever loses his life for the Gospel shall save it to life eternal.

1. We cannot follow after Jesus on the road to eternal life without carrying our cross after Him. It is useless trying to avoid it. If we fly from it in one shape, it will come to us in some heavier form. The wisest way, the only way if we desire peace, is to accept it willingly, to kiss that holy cross, the carrying of which is the sign that we are followers of our King along the royal road that leads to eternal life.

2. To each God allots a special cross intended to school him and fashion him to the likeness of his Master. It is often a very hard one to accept with submission and joy, but it will soon become lighter if we take it up ourselves, and consider the carrying of it a privilege, just as it will become heavier if we rebel against it. What are my dispositions in regard to the cross God has laid on me?

3. Christ demands of us a complete sacrifice if we are to be His. We must be ready to give up life itself at His command. Happy indeed is he to whom such a sacrifice is granted! Would that we were worthy of laying down our life for Jesus! O Christ! give me at least the loyal desire to sacrifice all to Thee!

Seventeenth Week: Tuesday.
Loss and Gain.
St. Matt. xvi. 26.

"What doth it profit a man if he gain the whole world and suffer the loss of his own soul? or what exchange shall a man give for his soul?"

1. The influence of the visible things around us is so great that it seems sometimes to obliterate the world invisible. Heaven and Hell are far away in the distance; and close at hand with its immediate offer of overpowering pleasure or riches or honour, is some tempting prize that attracts our lower nature or flatters our pride. Then it is that our lot is cast, and often eternity depends upon our calling to mind and acting upon these words of our Lord: "What doth it profit a man if he gain the whole world, and suffer the loss of his own soul?"

2. Our Lord does not merely say that we make a bad bargain if we accept worldly advantages to the eternal loss of our soul, but that the gain of all the world is as nothing compared with the smallest loss of grace in this world and of glory in the world to come. If we could enjoy unspeakable happiness for a million years and no longer, we should still be losers if thereby we forfeited any merit whatever in God's sight. What utter folly, then, to neglect any grace.

3. What exchange can a man give for his soul? *i.e.*, by what sacrifice of external things can he ensure his salvation? Nothing save humility and charity can purchase Heaven. Yet our Lord promises the Kingdom of Heaven to those who give alms liberally for the love of God, and to those who make any great sacrifice for His sake. In this sense we can, through God's mercy, purchase the Kingdom of Heaven for ourselves.

Seventeenth Week: Wednesday.
The Transfiguration.
St. Matt. xvii. 1—13.

Jesus takes Peter and James and John into a high mountain and there is transfigured before them, allowing the glory of His Divinity to shine through the veil of His flesh. Moses and Elias appear, and talk with Him of His approaching Passion.

1. Our Lord chose Peter, James, and John as representatives of the three virtues necessary for those who are to behold the glory of the Lord—loyalty, charity, and purity. These are the virtues which open the door of Heaven, and on earth admit those who possess them to a foretaste of happiness to come. If I had more of those virtues, I might hope for greater union with our Lord, and a larger share of the peace and joy that He imparts to those who cultivate them.

2. Why was our Lord transfigured before the chosen Apostles? It was chiefly to prepare them for the strain that His Passion and Death would put upon their faith in Him. It was to help them by the memory of His glory when they should see Him humbled to the dust. So God in His mercy gives to us a glimpse of the happiness reserved for us, before He tries our fidelity by desolation and suffering.

3. Moses and Elias appeared with Jesus, as the representatives of the Law and the Prophets. In the Son of God the Law was fulfilled, and all that the Prophets had foretold. None save He had ever perfectly obeyed the Jewish Law or their long expectancy. So to us the first sight of the Son of Man in His glory will make our time of expectancy on earth and in Purgatory seem as nothing in the intense joy.

Seventeenth Week: Thursday.
The Healing of the Boy who was possessed.
St. Matt. xvii. 14—17.

When our Lord returned to the disciples, He found a crowd gathered, and in the midst a boy who was possessed with a devil, and who had been presented by his father to the Apostles to be healed; but they had been unable to cast out the devil. Jesus told the father that if he believed, all things are possible to him that believeth. The man answered: "Lord, I do believe, help Thou my unbelief." Our Lord expels the devil, and commands him never to return.

1. The poor boy whom our Lord healed had suffered terribly from the devil who possessed him from his birth, though he himself was in no way to blame. If these were the results where there was no fault on the part of the person possessed, what may be the power of the devil to ruin those who by their own vices prepare a home for the Evil One in their heart?

2. The condition of the boy's cure was *faith*— "If thou canst believe." How many a grace and how many a cure of our spiritual infirmities we lose through the feebleness of our faith! We do not believe that God can heal us, and so we are not healed. All things are possible to him that believes. This is our Lord's promise, and He will not fail faithfully and generously to perform it.

3. The father's answer: "Lord, I believe! help Thou my unbelief," is a prayer most suitable for us. We are conscious of the feebleness of our faith, yet at least we know that if Jesus helps us we shall believe in Him as we ought. When doubts assail us, we should cry out, Lord, I believe! When we are inclined to doubt God's love for us, our words should be, **Help Thou my unbelief!**

Seventeenth Week: Friday.
The Tribute-money.
St. Matt. xvii. 23—26.

At Capharnaum the collectors of the tribute-money paid by the Jews for the expenses of the Temple, came to St. Peter, and asked whether our Lord paid the tribute. St. Peter answered that He did. Jesus afterwards reminded him that tribute is exacted of strangers, not of sons, and therefore the Son of God could not be liable to it. But to avoid scandal, He sent St. Peter to the sea, and told him that in the first fish he caught he would find a stater, which he was to pay for both of them.

1. Behold the gentle and kind way in which our Lord reproves St. Peter's hasty assertion that the tribute-money was due from the Son of God. He gently shows him why he was wrong, and then suggests the course to be adopted. In reproving others, how different we are! How bitter and harsh! how violent and impulsive! Seek to be more gentle. "A drop of honey," says St. Francis of Sales, "is worth a gallon of vinegar."

2. The Jews had no right to demand tribute-money of Jesus, nevertheless He paid it. He did not stand up for His rights, as we are prone to do; or insist on a principle; but to avoid offence gave in, and allowed His rights to be set aside. How unlike we are to the Son of God, when we fight for what we consider justice.

3. The piece of money in the fish's mouth was a wonderful miracle. It is a type of many by which our Lord has provided for the necessities of His servants. If you are in need of money for some good end, have faith in Him, and **He will provide it.**

Seventeenth Week: Saturday.
The Dispute among the Apostles.

St. Mark ix. 32—34; St. Matt. xviii. 1—5.

On the way to Capharnaum, the Apostles dispute among themselves which of them shall be greatest. Our Lord on their arrival asks them what they talked of by the way? They in shame are silent; then He takes a little child, and tells them that if any desire to be first, he shall be last; that they must become like little children if they are to enter into the Kingdom of Heaven.

1. The teaching of Jesus during three years had not taught them the primary lesson of humility. They disputed for predominance and for the first place. On us, too, alas! how little effect His teaching has had! How we strive to be prominent, to be first, to show ourselves off, to throw others into the background. Alas! alas! How little have we of the true spirit of Jesus!

2. Yet the Apostles knew when Jesus asked them the subject of their discourse that it was displeasing to Him. It was the old Adam in them fighting against what they knew to be His will. So too when I thus seek to be first, when I boast, when I resent the superior success of others, I know full well that my temper is hateful to my Master. O Jesus! root out of me that spirit of pride, make me willing to be last of all and servant of all.

3. Our Lord sets before them a model and a warning. The model is a little child, gentle, docile, forgiving, dependent, submissive. The warning is that any one who seeks to be first, shall by God's just judgment, be last. I will try and imitate this model, and remember this solemn warning.

Eighteenth Week: Sunday.
On Scandal.

St. Matt. xviii. 6—14.

The sin of scandal is spoken of by our Lord in words of more than usual severity. "Woe to that man by whom scandal cometh. It were better for a man that a millstone should be hanged about his neck, and that he should be drowned in the depths of the sea, than that he should offend one of these little ones."

1. What is scandal? It is any word or act tending to lead others into sin. We must not think that we have necessarily given scandal because others take amiss what we do or say, or because some harmless act of ours is the occasion to them of sin. But we give scandal when our actions are disedifying of their own nature, or tend to give rise to sinful thoughts or words or actions in those around us; then we are guilty of the sin of scandal.

2. What are the various kinds of scandal? The worst of all is when we do or say something with the express object of leading others to some sinful act. We also commit the sin of scandal when we do what we know is almost sure to lead to sin in others. We also give scandal when we do any act or say any word tending to lower the standard of those who witness it. Examine yourself whether you are guilty in any of these particulars.

3. Why is it that scandal is so awful a sin? Because he who gives scandal to others does the devil's work, and helps to drag others down to Hell. He has upon him the guilt not only of his own sin, but of any sin committed by those who through his deliberate fault, are led into sin by what he says or does. Better, says our Lord, that a man should die than give scandal. O my God, save me from the guilt of scandal.

Eighteenth Week: Monday.
On Fraternal Charity.

St. Matt. xviii. 21—35.

St. Peter asks our Lord how often we ought to forgive one who has injured us, and proposes seven times as the limit. Our Lord replies that we ought to forgive not seven times, but seventy times seven; and teaches by a parable that the mercy extended to us will be withdrawn if we do not show mercy to others.

1. The debt of the servant to his lord was ten thousand talents, a sum the vastness of which represents what we owe to God. Yet the servant does not despair of being able to pay his debt. Can we ever pay our debt to God? Yes, through His mercy we can, for Christ our Lord furnishes us with a treasure without limit on which to draw for our necessities; that store of supernatural graces which He purchased for us at the cost of His own precious Blood.

2. The servant to whom the debt is remitted meets a fellow-servant who has wronged him, and instead of having patience with him and forgiving him, he seizes him by the throat, and sends him off to prison, till he should pay his debt. So alas, we to whom God has forgiven so much, often will not forgive the comparatively trifling injuries done us. What base ingratitude! How mean is this unforgiving spirit, how different from the generosity wherewith God forgives us!

3. The unforgiving servant is treated by his lord as he had treated his fellow-servant. Can I accept this standard? Can I say from my heart, Forgive me my trespasses, in just the same way as I forgive those who have trespassed against me?

Eighteenth Week: Tuesday.
The Sacrament of Matrimony.
St. Matt. xix. 3—12.

The Pharisees ask our Lord whether it is lawful for a man to put away his wife for every cause. Jesus answers that it is never lawful, and involves the sin of adultery; that for those who can take it a life of celibacy for the Kingdom of Heaven is preferable to that of matrimony.

1. Before the coming of our Lord, the Jews' divorce was sometimes permitted. But our Lord declares that what God has joined together, no one is to put asunder. This indissolubility of marriage is one of the mainstays of the Christian household. With divorce there come in social corruption, neglect of children, laxity of morals, a break-up of the Christian family. Thank God for the dignity that Christ our Lord has given to the marriage contract.

2. In the Catholic Church, and there alone, marriage is a sacrament. It symbolizes the union of Christ and His Church. It is the mystical union of Christ with His Church that gives her her resplendent beauty, and makes her the spiritual mother of countless children. Pray that you may be a faithful child of Holy Church.

3. But honourable as matrimony is, there is a higher state of life. For those who are called to it, a life of chastity is a privilege and a grace surpassing that of the married state. Happy those who have such a vocation. They are indeed the favoured children of God. They must expect many trials and perhaps many temptations, but He who has called them will keep them safe. Pray for the grace necessary to do the will of God in that state of life to which He calls you.

Eighteenth Week: Wednesday.
The Feast of Tabernacles.
St. John vii. 2—23.

When the feast of Tabernacles drew near, our Lord's brethren, the sons of Mary of Cleophas, who did not yet believe in Him, urged Him to go up to the feast and openly make Himself known to the world. Jesus does not go up at once, but appears in Jerusalem about the middle of the festival. There is a great division of opinion among the Jews concerning Him.

1. It seems strange that our Lord's own relations, who had lived in constant intercourse with Him, should not recognize His true character. We learn from this, (1) That no one can know Jesus until the Holy Spirit enlightens him. (2) That the highest sanctity is something hidden and obscure. (3) That it is part of the spirit of the Gospel that a man's enemies should be they of his own family. May it not be that in your own circle there is some eminent servant of God of whom you think little?

2. Our Lord tells His brethren that the world hates Him because He bears testimony that its works are evil. This hatred of hearing the truth and of being found fault with is one of the marks of a worldly spirit. Do I resent reproof?

3. There are very various opinions about Jesus among the Jews. Some say, He is a good man. Others that He leads the people astray. What made the difference in their verdict? It was generally the state of their own hearts. Pride hates the truth; humility loves it. In proportion to my humility I shall love Jesus and all who teach His word.

Eighteenth Week: Thursday.
Our Lord in the Temple.
St. John vii. 14—20.

Our Lord comes into the Temple and teaches the people, who wonder at the learning of one who had never been instructed. He answers that His doctrine is not His own; that those who do God's will are alone competent judges of its true character.

1. The Son of God needed no human teacher. As man He was enlightened on everything by the Holy Spirit of God. So it is in their degree with the Saints of God. We find untaught men and ignorant women speaking and writing on abstruse theological subjects with perfect accuracy and the greatest wisdom. If I desire to write or speak of Divine things, I must continually look to Him.

2. But I must do more than this. We cannot penetrate into the mysteries of God unless we do His will. "If any man will do the will of God, he shall know of the doctrine." That is the way to attain to truth. Perfect obedience to God's holy inspirations. Then we shall receive a flood of light from Him.

3. There is a further step necessary. We must seek not our own glory, but God's. This is the test of the true messenger from Heaven, who carries the Divine message of love to men. "He that speaketh of himself seeketh his own glory." He that seeketh the glory of God, he is true, and he it is to whom God imparts a clear knowledge of truth. If I am blind, it is because I seek my own honour and glory instead of God's.

Eighteenth Week: Friday.
The Woman taken in Adultery.
St. John viii. 2—11.

The Pharisees bring to our Lord in the Temple a woman who had been taken in adultery, and after telling Him that Moses commanded that such should be stoned, asked His opinion. Jesus stooped down and wrote on the ground; and when they continued asking Him, replied: He that is without sin among you, let him first cast a stone at her. The accusers slink out ashamed, and Jesus dismisses the poor trembling woman with words of gentle kindness and counsel.

1. Observe the fierceness and righteous indignation of the Pharisees against this woman. Respectability was loud in condemning her. Is my spirit that of the Pharisees towards the outcast and fallen? Or do I pity them and long to help them to better things, and reflect that perhaps the worst of them is holier than I?

2. What did Jesus write upon the ground? It is said that each of the accusers read written there all his own sins against purity. No wonder that they were eager to escape. How should I like to have all the sins of my life written legibly for all to read? It would stop my railing tongue, which is full of indignation at the faults of others.

3. The poor woman trembling in the midst, awaited in terror the sentence of the Prophet of Nazareth. If these Pharisees had been so severe, what would be His severity? Yet from His Divine mouth there came no harsh words of reproach, but in gentle, loving, compassionate tones He sent her away consoled and forgiven. Do I show **a similar gentleness to the fallen?**

Eighteenth Week: Saturday.
The Man born Blind.
St. John ix. 1—41.

As our Lord passed by, He saw a man born blind. Calling him, He spat on the ground, and made clay of the dust and spittle, and spreading it on the eyes of the man, bade him go and wash his eyes in the pool of Siloe. The man obeyed, and was at once healed. He was afterwards excommunicated by the Pharisees, and our Lord, finding him, elicited from him an act of faith in His Divinity.

1. The Apostles asked our Lord whether this man's blindness was the punishment of his own sin or of that of his parents. Our Lord answered that it was neither the one nor the other, but that God's works of mercy might be manifested in him. We are never justified in attributing temporal calamities to sin.

2. Our Lord elicited no act of faith from the blind man as the condition of his being healed. Instead of this He tested him by obedience. The spirit of humble submission and unquestioning obedience is the surest way of obtaining graces from God. The prayer of him that humbleth himself pierceth the clouds, and those who are obedient to God wi l find that God listens to them in all that they desire of Him.

3. The Pharisees were indignant with Jesus because He had healed this man on the Sabbath, and with the man because He was loyal to Jesus. They cast him out of the synagogue in public disgrace. So many are now persecuted in one way or another because they are faithful to their consciences. But Jesus had not forgotten him, and He will never forget any who endure persecution for His sake.

Nineteenth Week: Sunday.
The Good Shepherd.
St. John x. 1—18.

Our Lord proclaims Himself the Good Shepherd who gives His life for the sheep and knows them all. He lays down His life of Himself, though at the same time He does so at the command of His Father.

1. The Good Shepherd makes the welfare of the sheep His first care. For this He sacrifices all His personal comfort and interests. For them He endures cold, hunger, peril, thirst, fatigue. For them He is willing to sacrifice life itself. What a picture is this of Jesus! He has the interest of each one of His flock so close to His Heart that for each He was willing to die. He seeks them in the desert whither they have wandered, dresses their wounds, carries them on His shoulders. O gentle Shepherd! may I appreciate Thy love for me, Thy poor wandering sheep!

2. He knows each one of His sheep, thinks of each, plans the welfare of each, gives to each sweet pasture and the water of life. He loves each far better than any loves himself, for He loves them with a Divine love. Why do I so often run counter to His love? What folly it is! He knows what is good for me, and loves me so fondly that the only limit to His love is the feebleness of my love for Him.

3. It is of His own accord that He lays down His life, for He chose voluntarily this life of subjection as Man. But this life once chosen, all His actions were done under obedience to His Father's command. This is the glory of a self-chosen life of obedience; it is a close imitation of the life of Christ on earth.

Nineteenth Week: Monday.
The Spirit of the Gospel.
St. Luke ix. 51—62.

When a village of the Samaritans refused to receive our Lord, because He was on His way to Jerusa'em, SS. James and John propose to call down fire from heaven upon them in punishment of their rejection of Him. Jesus rebukes them. "You know not of what spirit you are." The Son of Man is come not to destroy men's lives, but to save them.

1. These Samaritans refused to receive those whose faces were set to go up to Jerusalem. They hated the Jews and their Holy City. So now those who have turned their faces in the direction of the City of God are often rejected by the world. "No Catholics need apply." Those who are faithful to their conscience are driven out of house and home. Happy those who thus suffer for justice' sake!

2. SS. James and John are filled with indignation, and propose to invoke vengeance from Heaven on the evil-doers. They wanted to see them suffer as they deserved. This impulsive desire to bring down punishment on sinners is utterly opposed to the evangelical spirit. If we are thus angry with those who commit sin, it is not a good sign. It shows that we have the spirit of the Jews.

3. Our Lord rebukes the Apostles: "You know not of what spirit you are." Your spirit is the spirit of the Law; not the sweet, forbearing, indulgent spirit of the Gospel. Bitterness and indignant zeal destroys the souls of men; it strangles them from the birth. The Son of Man is come to save, not to destroy; to win by love, not to compel by terror. What is my spirit? Is it meek, humble, patient, gentle?

Nineteenth Week: Tuesday.
Some Conditions of following Christ.
St. Luke ix. 57—62.

As our Lord walked along He was accosted (1) By one who expressed a desire to follow Him whithersoever He went. Christ reminds him that this would involve poverty and a giving up of all the comforts of home. (2) By one who was willing to follow Him not at once, but after his father's funeral. Christ urged him to obey at once the call of God. (3) By another who desired to bid farewell to his relations before following Jesus. He is reminded that none who turn back are fit for the Kingdom of God.

1. The answer to the first of these brings out the spirit of poverty necessary to the followers of Christ. They must be ready to leave house and home, and to have nowhere to lay their head, to be destitute and forsaken by all, if God requires it of them. Should I accept those hardships if I knew that loyalty to God demanded it?

2. The second man asked what was good in the natural order. He desired to take care of his aged father until his death. But our Lord had called him: "Follow Me"—and to this call all else must yield. Here we have the necessity of obedience to the disciples of Jesus.

3. The third still clung to his home affections, and was not prepared to give them up at once for the love of Christ. The spirit of chastity requires that we should put away any sort of human affection which renders it impossible for us to give our hearts to Christ. He who casts longing looks after that which excludes the love of Christ, is unfit for the Kingdom of God. Christ will not brook a rival in our hearts.

J

Nineteenth Week: Wednesday.
The Mission of the Seventy.
St. Luke x. 1—6.

Our Lord about this time sent seventy of His disciples to preach in all the cities whither He was to go. They were commissioned with His authority, and those who rejected them would bring upon themselves judgment. Their mission was most successful, and the very devils obeyed their command. On their return our Lord warns them not to rejoice at this so much as at the knowledge that their names are written in Heaven.

1. The Apostles formerly sent out represented the Bishops of the Church; the Seventy represent the priests. Both carry the authority of Christ, and our Lord threatens the most terrible judgment on those who receive them not. Pray that you may never reject the voice of God speaking to you by the mouth of His priests, or by His holy inspirations, or by Holy Scripture, or the lives and writings of saints.

2. The Seventy had a joyful mission. What joy so great as that of co-operating with Christ in the salvation of men, and of seeing devils cast out from the heart of sinners as we urge them to penance? This is the pure and holy joy that belongs to those who labour and suffer for Christ, and begin even here to share His joy.

3. Yet there is a higher joy, and one which must come first of all in the hearts of those who love to serve Christ. It is the joy that comes from being united to Him in supernatural charity, and from the consequent conviction that we are destined, unless we should deliberately forsake Him (which God forbid), that our names are written in the Book of Life.

Nineteenth Week: Thursday.
The Good Samaritan.
St. Luke x. 25—37.

A lawyer asks Jesus what he must do to attain to eternal life. Our Lord answers that he must love God with all his heart and his neighbour as himself. In answer to the lawyer's inquiry, Who is his neighbour? our Lord tells the well-known story of the Good Samaritan, and elicits from this questioner the confession that it was the stranger, not the priest or Levite, who was the true neighbour to the man who fell among thieves.

1. Our Lord requires of us that we should love our neighbour *as ourselves*. This seems a high standard to ask of ordinary Christians, but nothing else will satisfy Christian charity. We must treat them as we should, under similar circumstances, expect that they would treat us. We must put ourselves in their place and act accordingly. Do I always observe this rule? Do I show charity to others where I should look for charity from them, and forgive them as I hope to be forgiven?

2. The Levite and priest had doubtless some excuse for passing on their way and leaving the wounded man in his distress. They were pressed for time; they had important business; the thieves might attack them if they lingered. We can always find excuses for the neglect of charity. Do I do so?

3. See the characteristics of the charity of this Samaritan. (1) He took great personal trouble. (2) Showed him the most tender care. (3) Sacrificed his own comfort, setting him on his own ass, and taking him to the inn. (4) Spending money freely. (5) Commending him to the care of others. Do I exercise a charity like his to all, even strangers, who come in my way?

Nineteenth Week: Friday.
Martha and Mary.
St. Luke x. 38—42.

At Bethany, Martha and her sister Mary used to entertain Jesus hospitably. Martha busied herself with much serving, but Mary sat at our Lord's feet and listened to His words. Martha came to complain to Him that her sister had left her to serve alone. Jesus answered, " Martha, thou art careful and troubled about many things. But one thing is necessary. Mary has chosen the best part that shall not be taken away from her."

1. Martha and Mary are the patterns of the active and the contemplative life. Both are admirable, and our Lord in no way rebukes St. Martha for her activity. But she was not satisfied with showing her own zeal: her complaint implies that her sister did wrong in not following her example. Are we inclined to blame those who spend their time in prayer instead of active benevolence? We should remember how our Lord rebuked Martha.

2. There was another imperfection in Martha. She was careful and troubled. She did not fulfil the condition given by Thomas à Kempis for an intimate friendship with Jesus: " Be peaceful and quiet, and Jesus will be with thee." We ought never to be "put out," never disquieted or troubled, when all things around us are not as we wish.

3. Mary sat at the Lord's feet and heard His word. Here is the secret of all sanctity: obedience to the voice of Jesus. This is the one thing necessary, this is what I must do: I must place myself before the Blessed Sacrament, pray for guidance and help, and listen to what Jesus says to me.

Nineteenth Week: Saturday.
How to Pray.
St. Luke xi. 1—13.

The Apostles ask our Lord how they ought to pray, and He gives them the Lord's Prayer as a form to be constantly used. He then illustrates the necessity of persistence in prayer by the parable of the man who desires to rouse his sleeping neighbour that he may give him some provisions for a friend.

1. The repetition of one prayer is not a vain repetition. It is the natural expression of an intense desire to be heard. Our Lord repeated over and over again His prayer in the Garden, and His prayer on the Cross: "Father, forgive them." If we are desirous of some grace, what can we do better than kneel before the altar and ask for it again and again?

2. The parable told by our Lord is a strong incentive to perseverance in prayer. We are to deal with Almighty God as a man who needs provisions at an unreasonable hour deals with his next-door neighbour. He knocks, and when refused knocks again and yet again; louder and even louder, until at length he obtains his request through sheer persistency. So we are sure to obtain our requests from God if we are sufficiently persistent.

3. God is pleased at such perseverance. He is not like men who are annoyed at such repeated petitions. He will give us a good gift of which the excellence will be increased not diminished by our continued requests. God delights to give good gifts to those who ask Him, and He will give the Holy Spirit to them in plenteous measure.

Twentieth Week: Sunday.
✠ The Divided House.
St. Luke xi. 14—24.

When the Pharisees accused our Lord of casting out devils by the aid of the prince of the devils, Jesus, seeing their thoughts, reminded them that such a division of the kingdom of Satan against itself would infallibly bring it to ruin, and that it is by the finger of God alone that devils can be cast out. The indwelling demon keeps possession in peace till a stronger than he takes away his armour and distributes the prey won from him.

1. Our Lord condescends to argue with some one who imagined that He expelled the devils from the bodies of men by some magic arts, derived from Satan himself. Satan would not be so misguided as to expel his own followers. Such a division of his kingdom against itself would soon bring it to nought. So we may be sure that those who exercise a beneficial influence on the characters of others and lead those with whom they are brought into contact to love virtue and forsake sin, are themselves actuated by good and holy motives and are doing the work of God.

2. "A house divided against itself shall fall." Unity of action is the secret of success. How many good works have been ruined by internal dissensions! Nay, it is impossible that any house or family or society can prosper, if it is divided against itself. Hence beware of grumbling, of ill-feeling, of party spirit, or of friendship for some to the exclusion of others.

3. Satan, the strong man, retained his dominion in peace until Christ, stronger than he, wrested his power from him. Now he lies crushed and feeble, full of malice as ever, but forced to relinquish his

Twentieth Week : Monday.
The Divine Maternity.
St. Luke xi. 27, 28.

While our Lord was addressing the crowd, a woman cried out, " Blessed is the womb that bore Thee, and the paps that gave Thee suck." But He said, "Yea rather, blessed are they that hear the word of God and keep it."

1. The woman who proclaimed the glory of Mary in being the Mother of God is a type of the Catholic Church, who rejoices to bear witness to the splendours of her Divine Maternity. It is Mary's relation to her Divine Son that is the source of all her perfections, and this title of Mother of God is necessary to safeguard our belief in the Divinity of her Son, and wherever it is set aside Jesus is neglected. In honouring her we are really honouring Jesus. O Mary, Mother of God, may we ever honour thee, and through thee Jesus our Lord !

2. Mary has a higher claim to be declared Blessed. The glory even of the Divine Maternity is subordinate to the glory of her unfailing obedience to every wish and command of Almighty God. This it is which exalts her to the highest place in Heaven. She was faithful to the will of God amid sorrows and desolation such as none but her ever experienced of all the creatures that God made. This is the glory of the creature—simply to carry out the will of the Creator.

3. To earn this blessing fully we must listen carefully for every word of God, and for every holy thought He whispers in our ears. We must also treasure them up as Mary did, often think of them, and pray that we may never have any rule of life save the holy will of God.

Twentieth Week: Tuesday.
The Rich Fool.
St. Luke xii. 13—22.

One of the crowd appeals to Jesus to speak to his brother that he may divide his inheritance with him. Our Lord refuses to interfere, and warns those present against covetousness, telling how a certain rich man proposed to himself many years of satisfied enjoyment of all the goods he had accumulated. God said to him, "Thou fool, this night do they require thy soul of thee, and then whose shall those things be which thou hast provided?"

1. There is nothing more dangerous to our salvation than a grasping, avaricious spirit. It grows with advancing age, and unlike other worldly pleasures, it loses not its zest as years go on. It has a fatal power to tie down the soul to earth, and make a man averse from heavenly things and from submission to God. Am I fond of money? or if I have no opportunity of money-making, am I fond of anything upon earth for its own sake and apart from God?

2. What folly is any attachment to money or goods or anything else upon earth? The moment of death arrives, and then what avail all earthly possessions? Nay, they are a curse to him who has trusted in them. O death, how terrible thou art to a man who has peace in his possessions!

3. The story of the rich fool was told by our Lord on the occasion of one asking Him to interfere between himself and his brother in respect of some disputed inheritance. Our Lord's refusal is a warning not to entangle ourselves with the affairs of others which do not concern us. How much mischief has been done by the meddlesome interference of well-meaning men!

Twentieth Week: Wednesday.
Watch!
St. Luke xii. 35—49.

To those who are always prepared for the coming of their Lord, and continually seeking to do His will, is promised in His Kingdom an almost incredible privilege. He will make them sit down to meat, and will minister to them Himself at the celestial banquet. On the contrary, those who do not carry out His will, though they know it well, will be beaten with many stripes.

1. "Blessed is the servant whom his Lord, when He cometh, shall find watching." To watch for any one implies that we are continually thinking of him, and looking forward to and preparing for his return. He who is watching when Christ shall summon him is one who has made His will the rule of his life, who often in prayer seeks to know His will, who bears Him continually in mind. Do I fulfil these conditions?

2. What a reward is promised to those who are found watching! Christ Himself will minister to their wants; He will make them sit down at the heavenly feast, and will treat them as those who had done Him a service. He will actually minister to them Himself, giving them rich draughts of the water of life, and feeding their souls with food which will contain all possible sweetness, and fill them with all possible joy. How trifling then will appear all the sorrows and trials of earth!

3. Those who are not watching, but taking their ease, with no care for their Master's command, will receive stripes in proportion to the clearness of their knowledge of what was required of them. What reason, then, have I to tremble, to whom so much light and grace has been given!

Twentieth Week: Thursday.
The Unfruitful Fig-tree.
St. Luke xiii. 6—9.

In the vineyard of a certain man was a fig-tree which for three years had borne no fruit, but only leaves. At length the owner bids the gardener cut it down, but he intercedes for it, that it may be spared for one year more, promising that he will dig around it, and spread dung about its roots. If it bear no fruit during the coming year, he will raise no further objection to cutting it down.

1. Every Christian performs a number of good works which may all be referred to one or other of two classes. Some are acts of natural virtue, beautiful perhaps and marking a healthy tree, but of no solid value in God's sight, receiving their reward here, not hereafter. Other actions are supernatural, informed by the grace of God, done for love of Him. These are the rich fruit, pleasing to God, which shall endure to everlasting life. Are all my good actions done from a supernatural motive? If not, they are mere leaves, showy but valueless, to be buried in the fall of the year.

2. The tree that year after year bears no fruit is cut down, while that which bears fruit is pruned that it may bring forth more fruit. As years go on, does the fruit I bear continually increase? Or is there a gradual diminution in the amount of it, and do I approach the time when our Lord shall say, "Cut it down, why cumbereth it the ground?"

3. How patient our Lord has been with me! How He has waited, hoping that before it is too late, I will begin to correspond to His grace, and work for Him and not for self! Grant me this grace, O Lord, beyond all other graces, that I may never neglect Thy grace, nor fail of doing what Thou dost ask of me!

Twentieth Week: Friday.
The Narrow Gate.
St. Luke xiii. 23—27.

When our Lord was questioned as to the number of the saved, He answered by urging His disciples to enter by the narrow gate, and warning them that many shall seek to enter, but in vain.

1. No one knows, save God, the number of the elect. It is no business of ours. What concerns us is the knowledge that if we desire to enter by the narrow gate that leads to life, we must exert ourselves, resist our inclinations, endure hardships, submit to the yoke, humble ourselves, and pray for the grace of God, without which none can be saved. Do I make such an effort as is necessary to win the Kingdom of Heaven?

2. It is useless to think that we can go on all our lives living for self and resisting the grace of God, and when we draw near to death, can offer a prayer which will undo the past, and open to us the gate of Heaven. We must knock now, if we desire to be heard, we must make friends now with the Master of the house, if we desire that He will then welcome us as His own; we must earn His gratitude now by our charity to others for His sake and by our submission to His will. Then and then only shall we meet Him with joy.

3. How terrible to hear Christ say, "I know you not!" Better a thousand deaths than that one word from the Lord of Heaven and earth. What would Jesus say of me now? Am I one of those of whom He would say, "I know My sheep, and am known of them"? Or would He say, "I know you not, depart from Me?"

Twentieth Week: Saturday.
On Self-Exaltation.

St. Luke xiv. 7—11.

Our Lord observing how those invited to a feast chose for themselves the highest places, exhorts them to sit down not in the highest, lest their entertainer afterwards request them to give place to others, but in the lowest, that they may have the honour of being invited to go up higher.

1. This struggle for the highest place was not limited to the Jews. It still is the ordinary law of society. All seek their own, and are unwilling to give way to others, and are pained if they are not treated with the honour that they think they deserve. The cause of their discontent and vexation is their pride, and love of self rather than of God.

2. Our Lord seems to set before His hearers a very low motive. He does not tell them to take the lowest place because they ought to regard themselves as worthy of it, but simply that so they may have glory before those at table, and may avoid the ignominy of having to move down. It would have been fruitless to put before them any lofty and exalted motive. So if we are not influenced to virtue by the love of God, at least our own interest will perhaps move us.

3. Christ's object was gradually to lead the Jews to something nobler. He knew that the practice of humility even from an inferior motive would lead on to a love of it for its own sake, and because it is pleasing to God. It is wonderful how soon any acts of virtue bring their own reward, and lead us to love virtue itself, and Him of whose beauty all human virtue is but a faint reflection.

Twenty-first Week: Sunday.
The Great Supper.
St. Luke xiv. 15—24.

Our Lord compares the Kingdom of Heaven to a feast to which many guests are invited. But they all excuse themselves on one plea or another: their host, angry at their refusal, brings in the poor and the feeble and the blind and the lame, to take their places at his table.

1. Our Lord invites all men to serve Him in one or another way. Some are called into the Catholic Church from heresy; others to the religious life or to the priesthood; others to a life of resignation under some great suffering. All these are summoned thus as a preparation for that Heavenly Feast which He intends in His own good time to bestow upon all who are obedient to His summons. God has invited me; have I obeyed His call?

2. There are many who do not like the Divine summons. The invitation involves the relinquishment of something to which their heart clings, money or position, or earthly affections, or self-will, so they excuse themselves. "It is impossible for me to obey because I have my business to attend to, or my relations to please, or my way to make in the world." Alas! how unhappy the lot of such. Have I ever rejected any such grace?

3. In place of those who reject the call of God, He sends His servants into the highways to bring in the poor and the lame and the feeble. Perhaps this is the way that I have entered His service. Some other refused a grace from God, and it came to me, unworthy as I am of such an offer. Anyhow the grace came to me, and through God's mercy I accepted it, and it has placed me where I am. How can I ever thank God as I ought for His wonderful mercy to me?

Twenty-first Week: Monday.
The Lost Sheep.
St. Luke xv. 1—7.

When the Scribes and Pharisees murmured at our Lord for consorting with publicans and sinners, He asked them whether a man who has lost one out of a flock of sheep does not seek the wanderer, leaving the rest in the fold, and bring it back with joy. So the Good Shepherd calls the Angels to rejoice over every sinner who does penance.

1. How our Lord loves sinners! He seems to find happiness in their company. He eats and drinks with them, He converses with them as their friend and comforter and the lover of their souls. For them not a harsh word, nothing but looks of compassion and love. O Friend of sinners, have mercy on me, a sinner.

2. But not all sinners does He thus befriend, only those who are conscious of their misery and lament over it and cast longing glances towards Him, and cherish amid all their sins at least a faint spark of hope that He will set them free. Then He fans that spark into a flame of love and delivers them from their chains, and brings them in humble penitence to His feet. Then it is that His Sacred Heart is full of joy. O Heart of Jesus! who can ever fathom the depth of Thy love for the sinner who does penance!

3. Jesus is not alone in His joy. All the Saints and Angels in Heaven rejoice with Him. He calls them together to sing a hymn of triumph over the return of the wanderer, and they rejoice one and all with joy unspeakable at the triumph of Divine grace. O Jesus, grant me the privilege of taking part in the Divine work of bringing sinners back to Thee!

Twenty-first Week: Tuesday.
The Lost Groat.
St. Luke xv. 8—10.

What woman, asks our Lord, who has lost one out of ten pieces of money, will not light a candle and sweep the house, and seek diligently, till she find it? And when she has found it, she calls together friends to congratulate her on finding the lost coin.

1. As the shepherd seeking the wandering sheep represents our Blessed Lord, so the woman searching for the lost groat represents His Sacred Spouse the Church. She laments over every sinner lost to grace and leaves no means untried to regain him. The Church of Christ regards the loss of a single soul as an evil of sufficient importance to occupy her whole thoughts until she has regained the treasure lost. We do not estimate as we ought the value of a soul and the irreparable evil of a single mortal sin.

2. What means does the woman in the parable employ? She lights a candle, since he that will be reformed and recover the grace of God must come to the light that his deeds may be reproved. She sweeps the house, for the dust and dirt of sin must be cleared away before there can be true penance, and she searches diligently as every sinner must do before he can recognize and confess his sins with due contrition. Ask yourself whether you search diligently into your heart and cleanse it from sin, and make use of the light that God gives to the children of the Church.

3. The Church rejoices exceedingly over every sinner doing penance, and calls on all the saints to rejoice with her. Every conversion to God adds to the joy of every saint in Heaven. What a privilege then to take part in the conversion of sinners to God!

Twenty-first Week: Wednesday.
The Prodigal Son: his Departure.
St. Luke xv. 11.

A certain man had two sons: and the younger said to his father, Give me the portion of goods that falleth to me. And he divided to them his substance. Not many days after, the younger departed to a far country and there wasted his substance, living riotously. After a time he began to be in want.

1. The beginning of the fall of the Prodigal Son was a desire for independence. He did not like the yoke of parental authority and the secondary position he held as the younger son in his father's house. He wanted to have his liberty and to be able to do as he liked. This is the beginning of every fall; secret pride making us unwilling to submit and to be thwarted and to do the will of others.

2. The consequence of this spirit of pride in the younger son was to make him restless and discontented. He was not happy in his father's house. He longed to be elsewhere. Restlessness is almost always a sign of pride; it is one of the marks of self-will; turbulence and inquietude are the forerunners of sin to come and moral ruin not far off.

3. The Prodigal starts on his life of independence. At first it is pleasant enough; he rejoices in his liberty; indulges his every fancy, satiates himself with pleasure. But it does not last long. The devil is a hard master, and the poor Prodigal finds himself miserable, in want, friendless, deserted. Thus it is that the world treats those who live for the world. God grant that I may never forsake my Father's house!

Twenty-first Week: Thursday.
The Prodigal Son: his Repentance.
St. Luke xv. 17—19.

The unhappy Prodigal is at last reduced to feeding swine for hire. In his misery he comes to himself and remembers the peaceful happiness of his father's house, and resolves to return and throw himself at his father's feet and say: "Father, I have sinned against Heaven and in thy sight."

1. The Prodigal, in the quiet solitude, begins to reflect. He resolves to go back, and humble himself, and ask to be received, not as a son, but as a servant. Observe (1) the advantage of a quiet time for prayer and supplication. (2) The contrast between the constant happiness of the humblest who serve God, and the misery that soon ensues to those who cast off His yoke. (3) The willingness of the Prodigal to humble himself. (4) The value of inferior motives as leading to virtue. The Prodigal's repentance arose primarily, not from love of father or home, but from his present misery. Apply each of these to yourself.

2. The first impulse of true repentance is to cast ourselves at the feet of him whom we have offended and beg for forgiveness. It is not enough to be sorry, but this sorrow must include hope of forgiveness and reconciliation. I, then, will go to the feet of Jesus in all my sorrows and sins, for I know He will not reject me.

3. The Prodigal loses no time. He arose and went to his father. Delays are dangerous. When the grace comes we must act on it, and the sooner the better. *I will arise;* this must be the motto of all who recognize their sin and weakness. I, too, with God's help, will arise from all that hinders my faithful service of Him.

K

Twenty-first Week: Friday.
The Prodigal Son: his Return.
St. Luke xv. 20—32.

When the Prodigal on his return approached his father's house, his father, seeing him in the distance, runs to meet him, falls on his neck, and kisses him. He will not hear his self-accusing words, but bids the servants bring the best robe, a ring for his hand, and shoes for his feet, and kill the fatted calf, that they may rejoice and make merry on the occasion of his return home.

1. The father of the Prodigal is watching for the return of the wanderer, and sees him a great way off. So God watches and longs for the sinner's return, and even before he has reconciled himself to God, He anticipates him with graces, and mercy, and consolation, and marks of His forgiveness and love. O, how gentle is the Sacred Heart of Jesus! We do not half understand its depths of love and compassion.

2. How is the returning Prodigal treated? He has the best of everything. (1) The best robe, the robe of justice to clothe him so that he may appear, not as a servant, but as a beloved son. (2) The ring of pardon to show that he is no longer the slave of sin. (3) Shoes to prevent his tender feet from being injured by the stones which lie in virtue's path. (4) A banquet of good things to celebrate his happy return.

3. The elder son, who had always been faithful to God, is angry at the welcome given to the Prodigal. So those who have not gone astray, because they have had no very strong temptations, are often hard upon those who have sinned. We must beware, for perhaps we shall find that they are preferred to us, and are really dearer to the Sacred Heart of Jesus, as St. Mary Magdalen was.

Twenty-first Week: Saturday.
The Unjust Steward.
St. Luke xvi. 1—12.

The steward of a rich man, being dismissed for lavish expenditure, goes round to the debtors of his employer and reduces the amount of what they owe. By this liberality, though with money not his own, he earns their good-will and the prospect of shelter when he is turned out of his stewardship.

1. We are all of us stewards of God, entrusted with what is not ours but His, to be used for Him, not for ourselves. We are all unjust stewards in that we have not done this, but have used what God has committed to us for ourselves, independently of Him, perhaps have wasted it on things that we knew were displeasing to Him; reading what He would not wish us to read, indulging in useless amusements and recreations.

2. To all the time must come when we shall have to give an account of our stewardship. What sort of an account should I have to give for my use of God's gifts? Would there not be waste here, and mal-expenditure there, and a selfish and dishonest adoption as our own of time and talents belonging to God? Can I face the day of account? *Quid sum miser tunc dicturus?* What shall I say then in answer to my Judge?

3. There is a means by which I may still ward off His anger, and that is by great liberality to others and especially to those who are poor and in want. Thus I can purchase to myself friends who will plead for me with God. Have I been a good friend to the poor for God's sake? Have I been generous with my alms? If so, I shall find that God will listen to their prayers for me and will be generous to me.

Twenty-second Week: Sunday.
On the Use of Riches.
St. Luke xvi. 9—12.

Jesus points out to His disciples that the unjust mammon or worldly riches are given us that we may by our use of it obtain true riches, and that we may purchase for ourselves with it admittance into everlasting dwellings.

1. Our Lord teaches elsewhere that it is very difficult for the rich to enter into the Kingdom of Heaven. Why, then, are they given to men? It is in order that they may so employ them, that they may barter them for treasure in Heaven. We sometimes see those who have spent their riches on building a church, represented as carrying the Church like a treasure in their hand. Worldly wealth spent for God, will be exchanged by Him into glory in Heaven to all eternity. Am I generous in contributing to such works?

2. Above all, those who have spent their money on the poor seem to receive a reward beyond the rest. Our Lord speaks as if the poor had the keys of the Kingdom of Heaven, and were able to admit those who for God's sake had bestowed their money according to their ability in relieving their necessities. Happy will those be who at the judgment have the poor to plead their cause! Have I done all I can to deserve the suffrages of the poor?

3. Our Lord speaks of those who use their riches well as being faithful in that which is least. What a contemptible thing money is in itself! but what a precious treasure if used well! It will purchase the true riches, *i.e.* the grace of God, that seed whence springs eternal joy in Heaven. What folly, then, to love riches, except for the sake of giving them away for God's sake.

Twenty-second Week: Monday.
The Rich Glutton.
St. Luke xvi. 19—31.

There was a certain rich man who feasted sumptuously every day, at whose gate was laid a beggar named Lazarus. The rich man died, and his life of luxury was requited with the torments of Hell. Lazarus died, and was carried by the angels into Abraham's bosom. In Hell the rich man begged that Lazarus might be sent with one drop of water to cool his parching thirst; but in vain.

1. What a warning against a life of selfish luxury! We do not read of any crime committed by the rich man. He simply lived a life of ease and comfort and present enjoyment. No self-denying charity; no deeds of mercy; no humiliation of himself; no penance; and therefore at the end of life the torments of Hell to all eternity. In my life how little penance! How much self-seeking and love of ease! Have I not reason to fear?

2. In Hell the rich man is punished in kind. His love of choice wines is requited by a tormenting thirst and a fire consuming his palate. For his life of luxury and ease, his purple and fine linen, he is enwrapped in the scorching flames. This law of retribution in kind is a terrible one; I must anticipate it. I am proud, and I must humble myself; I love comforts, and so I will mortify myself.

3. Abraham has no pity for the poor man in Hell. He tells him it is the lot he prepared for himself. We must learn the lesson, and pray God that we may have evil things in this life, if the good things we enjoy are to cost us the good things of Heaven. Pray to suffer here that so you may rejoice in Heaven.

Twenty-second Week: Tuesday.
The Raising of Lazarus.
St. John xi. 1—45.

When Lazarus fell sick, his sisters Martha and Mary sent to Jesus, saying, " Lord, he whom Thou lovest is sick." Jesus after two days starts for Bethany, and arrives there when Lazarus had been dead four days. Martha hastens to meet Jesus. Mary waits until she is sent for. Jesus approaches the grave, and cries aloud, " Lazarus, come forth ! " And he that was dead came forth still bound with the grave clothes.

1. The message sent by Martha and Mary is a model of prayer in trouble, especially in temporal trouble. They do not ask for anything, they simply state their needs. He likes us to tell Him our troubles, and if He delays, and seems to neglect us as He did Martha and Mary, it is that He may in the end perform a signal miracle on our behalf. I then will tell Him my troubles, and be content to leave it all to Him.

2. See the difference between the active Martha and the passive Mary. The former runs unbidden to meet Jesus ; the latter waits. It was Mary's grief that chiefly moved the tears of Jesus. He likes those who are passive until He calls them to act ; those who remain where they are until He summons them elsewhere ; those who wait for His inspirations, instead of following their own impulses. Am I one of these?

3. The raising of Lazarus corresponded in the physical order to the raising of the soul from the spiritual death of sin. The latter is a far greater miracle. How happy I should account myself if I have the privilege of taking part with Jesus in raising from the corruption and death of sin, **any of those souls for which He died.**

Twenty-second Week: Wednesday.
The Assembly of the Pharisees.
St. John xi. 46—54.

Some of the Jews present at the raising of Lazarus carried information to the Pharisees, who with the priests held a council, at which they determined on the death of Jesus. Caiphas, as High Priest, declared that it was expedient that one man should die for the people, and not that the whole nation should perish. After this, Jesus withdrew to a distant place with His disciples.

1. It seems strange that one of our Lord's most wonderful miracles should have made those who beheld it more hostile than ever. Yet so it is: those who have hardened their hearts against God are repelled, not attracted, by the marvels of His love. They only hate Him the more when they see clear proofs of His power. So we see evil men misinterpreting the simple faith, and charity, and devotion of the servants of God. Is this my spirit?

2. What was the motive of these men? Jealousy; a fear lest they should be overshadowed, and their credit diminished with the people. They cloaked this under a show of fear of the Romans. But their real motive was hatred of Jesus as a rival to their own influence. Beware of the selfish effects of an insidious ambition and jealousy of the success of others.

3. On occasion of the council in which it was decided to destroy Jesus, Caiphas, the High Priest, declared under Divine inspiration that it was expedient that one man should die for the nation. Strange that so wicked a man should be inspired by the Holy Ghost! But it was an official inspiration. God speaks even through wicked men when they hold some sacred office. How terrible a thing to have the Word of God in the mouth but not in **the heart!**

Twenty-second Week: Thursday.
The Ten Lepers.
St. Luke xvii. 11—19.

At the entrance to one of the towns through which our Lord passed, He was met by ten lepers who, standing afar off, cried, "Jesus, Master, have mercy on us." Jesus ordered them to go and show themselves to the priests, and as they went they were healed. One of them, a Samaritan, turned back to return thanks to Jesus, who was touched with his gratitude and dismissed him in peace.

1. The lepers standing far away were an example to sinners, (1) In their recourse to Jesus to be healed. (2) In their acknowledgment of Him as their Lord, and in their prayer for mercy. (3) In their obedience to His command to go and show themselves to the priests. (4) In their faith in so doing, even before they were healed. Admire their faith and confidence, and try to imitate it.

2. On the way to the priests they were healed. One of them, a Samaritan, could not refrain from turning back to thank his benefactor. Jesus loves the grateful: He will always bestow fresh blessings on those who are grateful for what they have already received. One who is thankless closes up the fount of Divine love and compassion. Hence learn very often to return thanks to God.

3. Our Lord was hurt at the neglect of the nine Jews. "Were there not ten cleansed?" He exclaims, "but where are the nine? No one has returned to give glory to God but this stranger." So those outside the visible Church may be far more grateful to God and dearer to Him than some within it.

Twenty-second Week: Friday.
The Unjust Judge.
St. Luke xviii. 1—8.

There was in a city a judge who feared neither God nor man. To him came a poor widow, asking to be protected from one who had wronged her. At first he would not listen, but at length, wearied out with her importunity, he granted her suit. So we must be importunate with God, for will He not avenge His own elect who cry day and night to Him?

1. When our Lord desires to impress upon His hearers any truth, we find Him often employing some unexpected and almost anomalous simile. Here He compares Almighty God to an unjust judge overcome by importunity. God loves importunity. We need never fear lest we should weary Him. He waits to be wearied by our petitions, and often requires this unbroken persistency as the condition of granting them. Do I thus persevere in asking for what I need?

2. The poor widow's cry was: "Avenge me of my adversary." Our cry must be the same. But of what adversary? Not of human foes, nor of those that treat us ill. Our prayers respecting them must be: "Father, forgive them." If we pray against them, God will hear our prayer only by visiting on us the misfortunes we invoke on them.

3. But there are very real adversaries against whom we should pray. (1) The devil, who tempts us, and seeks to bring us down to Hell. (2) Our predominant passion, whatever it may be. (3) Self, that is so continually asserting itself against God to our grievous harm, and is our worst enemy, which mars our happiness and destroys our peace. O God, I cannot fight against these alone! In Thy mercy, help me in the conflict.

Twenty-second Week : Saturday.
The Pharisee and the Publican.

St. Luke xviii. 10–14.

Two men went up to the Temple to pray, a Pharisee and a publican. The Pharisee thanked God that he was regular in the performance of his religious duties, and not like other men, unjust and impure, nor like the publican in the distance. The publican did not lift his eyes to heaven, but cried, "God be merciful to me a sinner!" The latter went away forgiven; not so the Pharisee.

1. The Pharisee's prayer was in some respects an excellent one. He returned thanks to God for the graces he had received. But he spoilt all by his pride, which caused him to prefer himself to others. God will not hear the prayers of the proud; He abhors them. Pride effectually bars the way against our receiving from God the graces which we need.

2. The publican's prayer was a prayer of humility. It recognized his own vileness, his dependence on God, his need of His mercy. This is the sort of prayer that God loves; it pierces the clouds and brings down a shower of graces. God cannot resist any one who really humbles himself. If I want my prayer to be heard, I must make certain that I pray with humility.

3. The chief end of this parable is to teach us the folly of despising any one. The very fact that we do so places us in the sight of God beneath the person we despise. Woe to us if we indulge the thought, Whatever I may be, I am better than so-and-so. If we could see ourselves as God sees us, we should perhaps perceive that we are really far worse.

Twenty-third Week : Sunday.
The Necessity of Humility.
St. Mark x. 13—16.

When little children were brought to Jesus, and the disciples sought to turn them away, Jesus was much displeased, and said : " Suffer little children to come to Me, for of such is the Kingdom of Heaven. For whosoever shall not receive the Kingdom of God as a little child, shall not enter into Heaven."

1. Jesus was displeased with those who sought to keep away the children from Him. Children are very dear to Him. He loves their guilelessness, innocence, simplicity. He watches over them with jealous care. Woe to those who injure them or neglect them, or indulge them unwisely, or set them a bad example. As the privilege of bringing them up is very great, so also is the responsibility.

2. The reason Jesus gives why the children are to be brought to Him is that "of such is the Kingdom of Heaven." What can be higher praise than this? He likens children to the Angels of God. He says that they are the nearest counterpart on earth of the Saints in Heaven. O blessed privilege of little children ! How different is their obedience and humility from my perversity and pride !

3. No man shall ever enter into Heaven unless he receives on earth the Kingdom of God as a little child. What does this mean? It means that we must put our neck willingly under the yoke as children do, that we must be docile as children are, that we must have a sense of continual dependence on God as children depend on their parents, that we must look to Him in every need, as they do to their elders. Am I childlike in these respects, or am I stiff-necked and stubborn and independent?

Twenty-third Week: Monday.
The Rich Young Man.

St. Mark x. 17—27.

A young man came and asked, "Good Master, what shall I do that I may receive life everlasting?" When Jesus answered that he must keep the commandments, the young man assured Him that he had done so from his youth. Then Jesus said, "One thing is wanting to thee; sell all thou hast, and give to the poor, and come and follow Me." Then the young man departed in sorrow, for he had great riches, and was not willing to abandon them.

1. The rich young man had always lived a good and upright life, so that our Lord loved him. But there came to him a further grace. Jesus invited him to give up his riches and follow Him. So with the hearts of those who live a life of obedience to God's law, higher graces always are given, to be generous with God as well as to fulfil the law of justice.

2. But unhappily for him he had great possessions, and these had gradually been gaining dominion over his heart; and when our Lord called him, and there came to him the grace to give up all for God's sake, he turned away sad, and would not give them up. O how great is the danger of a man whose heart clings to his possessions! God grant that my heart may not cling to any earthly good.

3. For all there is at some time a decisive crisis, a choice between treasure on earth and treasure in Heaven. Alas for those who at such a crisis fail of the grace given them, and reject the secret inspiration! Help me, O God, when such a time comes to me; may I always listen to Thee and follow Thee!

Twenty-third Week: Tuesday.
The Evangelical Counsels.
St. Matt. xix. 23—30.

When the rich young man had departed, our Lord dwelt on the difficulty of salvation to the rich. In answer to St. Peter's inquiry what reward would be given to those who leave all and follow Christ, our Lord promises a hundred-fold in this life, and in the world to come life everlasting.

1. Why is it so difficult for the rich to be saved? Because riches tend to make a man lose his sense of dependence. Is it impossible for the rich to be saved? Certainly not. The power of God can do anything; it can make a camel pass through the eye of a needle, and it will enable a rich man to become detached from his riches and escape the fatal peril of trusting in them. If we are rich, let us beware of the danger that riches involve; if poor, let us thank God that we are free from it.

2. But there is one means of escape, and only one. He must make some sacrifice by way of generous alms if he wish to die a happy death, and to escape the enthralling influence of wealth. But those to whom God gives the grace of a complete relinquishment of their possessions will have a far larger reward.

3. What is this reward? It is the gift of a far greater and higher happiness than they could ever have attained from their wealth, and in Heaven the certain promise of everlasting life. This will be the recompense of all who have given up anything, whether great or small, for Christ's sake; for He looks to the generosity of heart, not merely to the external act.

Twenty-third Week: Wednesday.
Coming Troubles.
St. Matt. xxiv. 4—11.

Our Lord predicts to His disciples many sorrows before His return to judge the world. There are to be wars, famines, and pestilences. False prophets are to arise and to seduce many. Those faithful to Christ are to be hated, afflicted, persecuted, and put to death.

1. The history of the Church of Christ is anything but a series of triumphs. It always has been and always will be persecuted, first in one country and then in another; and as the end draws near, persecution will be more cruel, more subtle, more persistent than ever. The Immaculate Bride of Christ must share the fortunes of her Spouse. It is a mark of her union to Christ that she has to suffer with Him. Rejoice in being a child of the suffering Spouse of Christ, and not of the bedecked and bedizened queens that hate her, persecute her, and seek in vain to imitate her matchless beauty.

2. As time goes on, false prophets will arise and will lead many astray. False Reformers, Revivalists, Gospel Evangelists, servants of the State who place it above the Church, or seek to sever it from her dominion. What a countless multitude of those servants of Satan! Alas, how many they have seduced! Thank God you are not of them.

3. Apart from persecution by wicked men, the faithful children of the Church will always have to suffer. First one trouble, then another—sickness, sorrow, poverty, humiliations—these are the friends in painful guise that lead us to Heaven. Courage, then! If we patiently suffer with Him now, we shall one day reign with Him in glory.

Twenty-third Week: Thursday.
The Signs of His Approach.
St. Matt. xxiv. 10—12.

Three signs will manifest the time of our Lord's second coming. (1) Many shall be scandalized. (2) Charity shall grow cold. (3) Iniquity shall abound.

1. To be easily scandalized is always a sign of a falling away from the love of Christ. "Blessed are they that love Thy law," says the Psalmist, "they shall not be scandalized in it." They know their own good-will and honesty, and they attribute the same to others. On the contrary, those who are themselves weak in virtue, are always talking scandal to what they see around them, and imputing bad motives. To which class do I belong?

2. Charity shall grow cold. The first fervour of the Christian Church did not last long. When prosperity and wealth and power fell to her lot, her children began to grow cold in their charity. There are sad periods in the history of the Church. God in His mercy never forsook her, and sent holy men to renew the waning love and zeal of Catholics. But as the end draws near, there will be a sad falling away. When I look over my own history, is it like that of the Christian world—first fervour, then coldness? Alas, I fear it is; at all events, I have not advanced in fervour as I ought.

3. Iniquity shall abound. When we look into the modern world, we recognize this sign of our Lord's approach. Under a fair guise, how much hidden vice, how much secret pride! What selfishness! What forgetfulness of God! In my heart there is, alas, a similar festering sore under what is perhaps a fair exterior,

Twenty-third Week: Friday.
The Suddenness of His Coming.

St. Matt. xxiv. 37—44.

The second coming of the Son of Man is to be sudden and unexpected, like the Flood in the days of Noe. Hence the necessity of continual watchfulness.

1. The Church of Christ has always been expecting the coming of our Lord. St. Paul speaks of it as very near at hand. In the Apocalypse of St. John, Christ says, "Behold, I come quickly." In the early ages and the middle ages of the Church, there has been a continual expectancy of His speedy return. This is a recognition that He will come when we do not look for Him. I therefore must be ever expecting Him if I would not be taken by surprise.

2. The world will go on with its business and pleasures just as usual up to the moment when the Archangel's trumpet shall summon men to judgment. As before the Flood, they will eat and drink, and marry and be given in marriage, as if the world was going to last for ever. So the world acts now. Who would think that they will in a few years, one and all, have to give a strict account of every deed and word and thought? Is not my life in this respect too much like that of the thoughtless world around?

3. Watch. This is the soldier's motto, and must be the Christian's. Watch against temptation; watch against occasions of sin; watch for your Lord's coming. Do you not already see in the horizon signs of His approach, tokens that you have not long to wait before your turn will come? Be ready, then, for you know not when the Son of Man shall come.

Twenty-third Week: Saturday.
The Labourers in the Vineyard.
St. Matt. xx. 1—16.

Our Lord describes the Kingdom of Heaven as like to a householder, who goes out at various times in the day, and invites those who are standing idle to go and work in his vineyard. In the evening he gave the same pay to all.

1. At various periods of life God calls men to serve Him. Sometimes in early life He binds them close to Him. Sometimes He leaves them half their days without any extraordinary graces or special inspirations. Sometimes in old age the light comes which never shone before. God gives at some period some special inspiration to labour for Him. We must listen intently for the voice of God speaking to us. All our happiness depends upon our obeying His call.

2. God gives the same reward to those who have laboured for a long or for a short time, if the latter obeyed His voice as soon as they heard it calling them. To all in Heaven He will give the same recompense of the Beatific Vision; but the degrees of bliss will depend on faithfulness to grace. Those who lived but ordinary lives in the world, or were pagans or Protestants half their days or more, will have the same reward as those who consecrated themselves to God from childhood, if they had the same graces at last, and were equally faithful to them.

3. In the parable some are displeased at the privileges of others, and insist on their own fancied right to receive more than they. Such jealousy is hateful in God's sight. If God in His Divine generosity gives to others unearned gifts, we should rejoice in their happiness.

Twenty-fourth Week: Sunday.
The Petition of the Sons of Zebedee.
St. Matt. xx. 20—23.

SS. James and John come with their mother to our Lord, asking for the privilege of sitting next Him in His Kingdom. Jesus answers that they do not know what they ask, and inquires whether they are able to drink of His chalice? They say: "We can." Jesus tells them that they shall do so, but that the first seats in His Kingdom will be given to those for whom they are prepared by His Father.

1. The request of the sons of Zebedee seems to have been the outcome of love for Christ, mingled with ambition. Ambition is a good thing if it is not a selfish or worldly ambition, but an ambition to be high in the ranks of those who love God and are loved by Him, and so to be nearer to the Sacred Heart of Jesus. This should be our constant aim, to deserve a high place in the assembly of the lovers of Jesus.

2. The condition of a high place in the love of Jesus is a large share in His sufferings. All who are His dearly-beloved here are to drink of His chalice. If Christ were to ask us, Can you drink of the chalice that I drink of, the chalice of neglect, of outrage and contempt and unkindness, of interior darkness and a death of agony, could we answer generously, as did James and John, Yes, Lord, we can, not by our strength, but by Thy grace?

3. The high places in Heaven are to be given not to those who merely ask for them, but to those who deserve them. They are reserved for those who hear the Word of God, and do it; for those who amid the difficulties and hardships, persevere in obedience to God and loyalty to Him. Am I such?

Twenty-fourth Week: Monday.
The Blind Men of Jericho.
St. Matt. xx. 29—34.

As Jesus went out of Jericho, followed by a great crowd, two blind men who sat begging by the roadside cried out, "Jesus, thou Son of David, have mercy on us!" Then Jesus stood still, and asked them what they desired. On their replying: "Lord, that our eyes be opened," He touched their eyes, and at once they saw and followed Him.

1. Try and picture the scene. A great crowd following Jesus and these two blind men shouting: "Jesus, have mercy upon us!" See Jesus listening, stopping, speaking to them, and learn from this that He never loses sight of any individual in the crowd. He has thoughts of love and plans of mercy for me. If I cry loud enough, He will stop and listen, and hear and answer my petition.

2. The prayer of these two blind men was that their eyes might be opened. How sadly we need that our blindness should be dispelled by Jesus! Our sins have gathered like a mist around our eyes. We cannot see the beauty of holiness and the hideousness of sin, and the happiness of serving God. Open my eyes, O Lord, to see all this, that so I may forsake my sins and serve Thee with my whole heart.

3. When those blind men recovered their sight at Jesus' touch, at once they followed Him. This should be the effect of all the mercy Christ has shown me, and the graces He has lavished on me. I must follow Him more closely, more obediently, with a greater desire to imitate Him, to love Him, to suffer with Him even unto death.

Twenty-fourth Week: Tuesday.
The Conversion of Zaccheus.
St. Luke xix. 2—10.

Zaccheus, a chief among the publicans, climbed into a sycamore-tree that he might see Jesus as He passed. When Jesus came to the place He looked up, and bade Him descend, as that day He would lodge in Zaccheus' house. Zaccheus on the occasion of Jesus' visit, gave half his goods to the poor, and offered four-fold restitution to any he had wronged.

1. Our Lord's Heart is always won by those who take trouble for His sake. Ascetical writers teach us that the sycamore-tree is an emblem of the Cross, because suffering is necessary to solid progress in virtue, and that Zaccheus climbing into it was an instance of one who accepted the folly of the Cross, which is the truest wisdom for those who long after an intimate union with Jesus.

2. Jesus espied Zaccheus in the tree. He promises that He will be his guest, publican and sinner as Zaccheus was. So he is always ready to come and be our guest in Holy Communion, if we (1) long after Him as Zaccheus did, (2) obey His word, (3) are prompt in following His inspirations, (4) count it a joy and happiness to have Him for our Divine Guest.

3. Observe the effect of our Lord's presence in his house. (1) The avaricious publican gives half his goods to the poor. (2) He promises four-fold restitution if any one has anything against him. Thus it is that our Lord enables us to expel from our souls even the most deeply rooted and inveterate faults.

Twenty-fourth Week: Wednesday.
The Lord and his Servants.
St. Luke xix. 11—28.

A nobleman about to leave his home for a time gives his ten servants each a pound with which to trade for their master. On his return he finds that one has gained ten, another five pounds. But one of them had kept the pound wrapped up in a napkin. The lord rewards the faithful servants and condemns the one who had made nothing.

1. These pounds are the graces that God gives to us gratuitously. They are not purely a gift, but a gift that carries with them a serious responsibility. This is true of all God's gifts: health, strength, money, success, and above all, supernatural graces. We have to answer for each; they are given to us to trade withal for our Master's glory. If we are not our own, much more the gifts God has put into our hands are not our own but His. Do I use them with this fact ever before my eyes?

2. The pounds traded with produced more pounds. So God's graces if rightly used produce fresh graces. Our Lady's immeasurable grace was the result of her invariable faithfulness to grace. If I want more grace from God, the only way to obtain it is to make a faithful use of the graces I possess.

3. Notice the magnificence of the reward; a city, in reward for a pound well used. Notice also the exact proportion between the sum acquired and the dominion granted. In Heaven our reward will be magnificent beyond our highest expectations, but always in proportion to our faithfulness to grace during our time of probation.

Twenty-fourth Week: Thursday.
The Procession of Palms.
St. Luke xix. 29—38.

When our Lord approached Jerusalem, a great multitude went out to meet and welcome Him. Some spread their garments in the way, others strewed branches on the ground, and the children cried, "Hosanna to the Son of David." Among them rode our Lord, seated on an ass, meek and humble of heart, with mingled sentiments of joy and sorrow.

1. The entry into Jerusalem was the occasion on which the multitudes openly recognized Christ as their King, as coming with authority from God Himself. The palm branches were their testimony that He had triumphed over His enemies; the garments strewn in the way was their declaration of submission to Him; and the cry of Hosanna was the prayer that God might prosper Him in His Mission. Rejoice in this recognition of His Divine authority, of His triumph over His enemies, of your subjection to Him, and to others for His sake; and pray that His Kingdom may be spread over the earth more and more.

2. In the midst of all this pageant rode Jesus, meek and humble, mounted on an ass. Those plaudits of the multitude, how little they affected Him; yet He rejoiced in their loyalty, and in their good-will. Pray that in the midst of applause you may be meek, as He was.

3. Mingled with His joy was a bitter sorrow at the knowledge that in a few days, the fickle crowd would shout: "Crucify Him!" He anticipated the scene close at hand, when those He loved would reject Him and desire His death. Learn of Him to see the worthlessness of popularity, **and be willing to bear reproach with Him.**

Twenty-fourth Week: Friday.
Christ weeps over Jerusalem.
St. Luke xix. 41—44.

As our Lord drew near to Jerusalem, He began to weep over it, and to say: "If thou hadst known, and that in this thy day, the things that are to thy peace! But now they are hidden from thine eyes." He then foretold the coming destruction of the city.

1. Jesus, looking down upon the city of Jerusalem, was full of sorrow at the thought of its approaching doom. He loved Jerusalem, and His own nation. Loyalty to our country is a duty to God, as well as an instinct of the human heart. Every good man is a patriot. But our patriotism must be a desire above all that our land and city may be faithful to God, not merely that it may be great among the nations of the earth.

2. The cause of the grief of Jesus was the thought of what Jerusalem might have been, as compared with what it was. Alas, over how many cities He may well weep now! What might they have been if their rulers had been faithful to God, and what are they—London, Paris, Vienna, the once Christian city of Constantine? What awful paganism, luxury, corruption, pride! We ought to pray for the nations thus robbed of their inheritance by heresy and sin.

3. Over many an individual too our Lord utters the same mournful words: "If thou hadst known!" If only thou hadst listened to the secret inspirations of grace, thou mightest have been a saint; and now——. Grant, O Lord, that my ears may not be deaf to the things that make for my eternal peace!

Twenty-fourth Week: Saturday.
On Death to the World.

St. John xii. 20—25.

On the occasion of certain Gentiles desiring to see our Lord, He answers that the time is at hand when He is to be glorified over the whole world. Before this He must be like a grain of wheat, which, unless it die, remains alone; but if it falls into the earth and disappears, it brings forth much fruit.

1. During our Lord's Ministry He had instructed His Apostles not to go into the cities or ways of the Gentiles. But now a new era is at hand, and the Son of Man is to be glorified by Gentiles as well as by Jews. The Gospel of Christ is all-embracing. There is place for all in the Kingdom of Heaven. Thank God for the universality of the Church, and pray that you may find a place in it.

2. Our Lord's glory and the spread of His Kingdom is only to be attained by His death. He is that Divine grain of wheat which falls into the barren earth and makes it to fructify by His Passion and Crucifixion. This law of the humiliation and annihilation of self as the condition of future glory and success in work for God extends even to Jesus. How much more is it necessary for sinful men!

3. This is the fact that I must face. I must die to myself and to the world if I am to take part in the spread of Christ's Kingdom. I must practise unselfishness, be willing to be overlooked and forgotten, live a hidden life, suffer and be subject. Is this my temper, or do I want to be prominent and highly esteemed?

Twenty-fifth Week: Sunday.
The Barren Fig-tree.
St. Matt. xxi. 19.

Jesus walking one morning into Jerusalem and being hungry, seeing a fig-tree on the way, came to seek figs on it. Finding none, but leaves only, He said, " May no fruit grow on thee henceforward for ever." And presently the fig-tree withered away.

1. The fig-tree was a symbol of the Synagogue of the Jews, sightly enough and apparently flourishing, but wholly destitute of fruit. External rites and ceremonies, long prayers for ostentation's sake, alms given from natural benevolence or for show, and not with a supernatural motive, were the general characteristics of the Jews of our Lord's day. The same dangers still exist. We may easily spoil what we do by our vanity and love of self, and so produce only leaves, not fruit.

2. It was not yet the time of figs. But the time is always present of bringing forth good fruit to God. It is dangerous indeed to say, the time has not yet come for me to devote myself to God; to-morrow, or at some future time, I will listen to His inspirations, for this time may never come.

3. The time of figs never came to the fig-tree in this parable, for Christ's malediction left it powerless to bring forth fruit. How sad would be my lot if such a curse were to fall on me. Christ is very patient, but the time may at length come, if I do not bear fruit, when He will say: From thee no fruit henceforward! I must be up and doing; working not for myself, but for the honour of Christ Jesus my Lord.

Twenty-fifth Week: Monday.
On Confidence in Prayer.

St. Mark xi. 22—24.

When the disciples observed that the fig-tree had withered away at our Lord's word, He takes occasion to urge the importance of confidence in prayer. "Whatever you shall ask in prayer *believing*, you shall receive. Whoever shall have faith as a grain of mustard-seed, if he shall say to a mountain, Take up and cast thyself into the sea, it shall be done."

1. Confidence is no less a requisite in prayer than persistence and humility. Men are much more ready to grant the petitions of those who approach them with a respectful boldness. So it is with God. He likes us to assume as a matter of course that we shall be heard. Do I come with this confidence before God, to ask what I need?

2. Why is it that we have so little confidence? It is not that we doubt the power of God, or even His goodness. It is not the fact of our past sins. It is our present love of self. It is the want of perfect conformity to His will that saps our confidence. We hold something back which we have not given with all our heart to God. We are not generous with Him, and so we naturally conclude that He will not be generous with us.

3. What ought to be the ground of our confidence? The love of Jesus for every one who is a member of His Spouse the Church. He cannot help loving His immaculate Spouse and every member of it. "He loved me, and gave Himself for me." We always feel at our ease with those who we know love us, and none loves us like Jesus. Hence we should be at our ease with Him, and this confidence will obtain all we ask.

Twenty-fifth Week: Tuesday.
Our Lord's Authority to Teach.
St. Matt. xxi. 23—27.

When the Chief Priests and Ancients questioned our Lord as to His authority to teach, He asked them in reply whence John the Baptist derived his authority? This question they could not answer. Our Lord answered that as they could not tell, so neither would He tell them whence His own authority was derived.

1. This question of the Chief Priests was a clear mark of their hatred of the truth. They had seen in Jesus marvels that God alone could work, and had heard from His lips words which God alone could inspire. Yet they objected to His teaching on the ground that He had received no commission to teach. We can always raise objections to the actions of those we dislike and regard with an evil eye. We question their authority and dispute their power.

2. Selfishness and jealousy of others always defeats its own end. The Ancients and Pharisees, by keeping aloof from St. John, and refusing to acknowledge his Divine mission, were furnishing a weapon that our Lord turned against themselves. They had hated John and had rejected his teaching, yet they dare not deny his authority to be from God. So it always is with the selfish: while seeking to secure their own interests, they are their own worst enemies.

3. When men came to our Lord as humble searchers after truth, He never left them in doubt as to His claims on their allegiance. But the Chief Priests had forfeited grace; their eyes and ears were closed to the truth. O unhappy condition! What more hopeless? May God in mercy save me from it.

Twenty-fifth Week: Wednesday.
The Disobedient Sons.
St. Matt. xxi. 28—32.

"A certain man had two sons, and to the first he said, Son, go work to-day in my vineyard. He said, I will not; but afterwards, moved with repentance, he went. The second answered, I go, sir, and went not. Which of these two," asks our Lord of the Priests and Ancients, "did the will of his father?" When they answered, The first, He tells them that the publicans and harlots will go into the Kingdom of Heaven before them.

1. The elder son in the parable was by no means a dutiful child. He refused to obey his father's command, but afterwards he repented and obeyed. I resemble this son in his early disobedience. Many and many a time God has ordered me or asked me to do something for Him, and I have virtually said, I will not. Have I since repented of my disobedience, and does He ever ask of me now some little act of charity or self-denial or humility, and do I answer in my heart, I will not?

2. The second son was a fair-spoken man, yet in his heart he was determined to follow his own will, not his father's; and in spite of his promise, he never obeyed the command given him. Am I not too much like him? In my prayers I say beautiful things to God. But when it comes to practice, I do not even attempt to carry out His inspiration.

3. The Pharisees in their pride fancied they were on the high-road to Heaven. What can they have thought of our Lord's words: "The publicans and harlots shall go into the Kingdom of Heaven before you"? I, too, who am so proud, must listen and hear our Lord saying the same to me; and I must humble myself accordingly, and see how much better they are than I.

Twenty-fifth Week: Thursday.
The Question of the Sadducees.
St. Luke xx. 27—40.

The Sadducees, who denied the resurrection of the body, asked our Lord whose wife a woman would be in the resurrection if she had been married several times on earth. Jesus answered that they were in error, not knowing the Scriptures, for in the resurrection none would marry, but all would live an angelic life. After this none of them dared to ask Him any more questions.

1. The Sadducees maliciously thought that they would puzzle our Lord by the objection they proposed to the resurrection of the body, and thus secure the double end of putting Him to shame and making His doctrine ridiculous. How vain their efforts! All the attacks of wicked men on God and truth will one day turn to their own confusion. We must be patient.

2. The Pharisees first misrepresented the teaching of Christ and then proceeded to demolish their own misrepresentation. So heretics misrepresent the doctrines of the Church—the Immaculate Conception, Eternal Punishment, Indulgences, Papal Infallibility, and the like—and then proceed to confute their own garbled version of the truth. Make an act of faith in the reasonableness as well as the truth of all that the Church teaches.

3. Our Lord tells the Sadducees that in Heaven all natural love will be swallowed up in supernatural. We shall love father, mother, brother, sister, wife, children, in God and for God, and not with any love that would interfere with others loving them too. Even in this world all our love for others must be unselfish if it is to endure.

Twenty-fifth Week: Friday.
The Vineyard and the Husbandmen.
St. Matt. xxi. 33—41.

A man had a vineyard which he let out to husbandmen. When the vintage drew near, he sent his servants to receive the produce due to him. But the husbandmen beat and ill-treated those who were sent, and killed some of them. At last he sent his son, saying, "They will reverence my son." But the husbandmen said, "This is the heir; let us kill him." What, asks our Lord, will the lord of the vineyard do to these wicked men?

1. The vineyard of the parable was the Jewish Church. To the Jews God sent prophets, whom they ill-used; and at last His own beloved Son, Whom they rejected, outraged, and put to death. What accounts for their extraordinary perversity? Pride, and the rebellion consequent on pride. We see it in the stories of Saul, Ahab, and others. Learn to hate pride.

2. Authority came to them at last in the form of the Son of God, meek and humble of heart, who went about doing good, whose gentleness and love won all men of good-will. Even Him they hated —nay, hated Him more than all because He spoke with paramount authority. Such is the result of pride. It tends to make us dislike even the authority that we know comes from Heaven. Grant me, O Lord, the spirit of submission and true humility.

3. Pride brings its own fall. Its short-lived triumphs are followed by its destruction and abasement. The Lord will come and crush the proud under His feet. He will drive them out from their inheritance. This is the story of apostasy from the truth: it is always pride. This is the reason why so many who begin well end miserably.

Twenty-fifth Week: Saturday.
The Wedding of the King's Son.
St. Matt. xxii. 2—13.

A king made a marriage-feast for his son, and invited many. But they neglected the invitation, and put to death those sent to invite them. Then the king being angry told his servants to go into the highways and call any they could find. When the king came to see the guests, there was one who had not on a wedding garment. The king ordered him to be bound hand and foot, and cast into the exterior darkness.

1. The feast to which God invites His guests is the feast of graces in this life and of glory in the next. How many He summons in vain! Those outside the Church He calls to enter in. Those living in the world He calls it may be to the religious life, or to some form of penance, or to a life of greater devotion. With those who refuse His invitation He is justly angry. O my God, I thank Thee that I have not substantially neglected Thy invitation!

2. Into the Church are gathered good and bad, so that it is filled with a variety of guests. So to the religious life it is not only the virtuous and holy that are called. Happy it is for me that God calls not the just only, but sinners also, else where would be my present privileges?

3. In the Catholic Church, even in the religious life, there may be some who have lost the wedding garment of charity. Alas for them, if the King comes while they are without it! Their lot will be exterior darkness for ever. I must be very careful not to forfeit the possession of this precious garment, or, if I should lose it, to regain it without delay by contrition and penance.

Twenty-sixth Week: Sunday.
Cæsar and God.
St. Matt. xxii. 15—21.

The Pharisees send their disciples with the Herodians to question Christ as to whether it is lawful to give tribute to Cæsar or not. He sees through their wiles, and, asking for a piece of money, elicits from them that the current coinage bears Cæsar's image upon it, and they are, therefore, to render to Cæsar what is acknowledged as his, and to God what is due to Him.

1. See the bitter malice of the Pharisees! How they hate Jesus! His holiness, purity, humility, charity, unselfishness were a reproach to their worldliness, impurity, selfishness, pride. I must be on my guard against a certain tendency to be jealous of those who are better than I am and are preferred to me. Instead of this I must try and imitate their virtues.

2. The questioners thought to show Christ either as a rebel or unpatriotic. But He utterly defeats them by His answer. Their acceptance of the Roman coinage was an acknowledgment of the Roman power, and therefore made it lawful, if not obligatory, to pay the tribute to Rome. Admire Christ's Divine prudence, and ask Him to give you the grace of prudent and unoffending words.

3. In the words, "Render to Cæsar the things that are Cæsar's, and to God the things that are God's," our Lord lays down the principle of civil and religious obligation. We must not neglect one for the other; both come from God. True religion can never make us unpatriotic or disobedient to lawful authority, and true patriotism and loyalty can never interfere with our duty to God and to the Church. But when the State goes beyond its proper sphere, then we must neglect all to obey God.

Twenty-sixth Week: Monday.
The Widow's Mite.

St. Mark xii. 41—44.

Our Lord sitting near the Treasury saw the people casting in their money, and many who were rich cast in much: a poor widow cast in a farthing. Jesus calls His disciples, and tells them that she has cast in more than all the rest, for she has given all she possessed to God.

1. Jesus watching the people casting the money into the treasury of the Temple was doing what He still continues to do, when there is a question of giving money for some pious end. He watches and sees what each gives, whether in the generosity of their heart they give the most they can, or whether they give, on the other hand, as little as possible. Which is my disposition when I am asked to give? Shall I obtain the large benediction that He bestows on the generous giver?

2. Yet generosity does not depend on the amount given, but on its proportion to the resources of the giver. To give a thousand pounds in charity may not be as generous a gift to God as to give a shilling or even less. We must give what will cost us something. If our charity is to be the pure gold that wins the heart of God, it must involve some self-denial.

3. The gift of the poor widow did more than cost her a slight self-denial. It left her penniless. How contrary her action to human prudence! But in the eyes of God it was the truest wisdom. What faith she must have had! What charity! No fear that she would be left in want. God would provide for her, and that most liberally, as He always does for those who are liberal with Him. Am I ready thus to give all to God?

Twenty-sixth Week: Tuesday.
The Great Commandment.
St. Matt. xxii. 35—40.

One of the Scribes asked our Lord, "Which is the great commandment of the Law?" He answered: "Thou shalt love the Lord thy God with thy whole heart and thy whole soul and thy whole mind. And the second is like to this : Thou shalt love thy neighbour as thyself. On these two commandments dependeth the whole Law and the Prophets."

1. The centre of all sanctity is the love of God. We must love Him with our whole soul and heart and mind. The affectionate loyalty of our hearts must be given entirely to Him, our bodies must be consecrated to Him, and our intellectual powers must be used for Him. Alas! how defective is my love and service ! Can I say that my heart is wholly fixed on God?

2. The second law of holiness is no less binding than the first. It flows from it and is inseparable from it. We must love our neighbour as we love ourselves. This is a very high standard, and few indeed are they who attain it. Yet it is what God requires. It is a command, not a counsel, that we should regard the interests of others as our own. This is the great lesson of Christ's life. To what extent have I learned it?

3. The obstacle to the keeping of these commandments is self-love. It prevents our loving God wholly, since He will brook no rival; and it prevents our loving our neighbour as ourselves, for it makes us postpone our neighbour's interests to our own. Yet this is fatal to all true self-love and self-interest. Those who forget themselves are those who alone promote their own interest and their happiness.

Twenty-sixth Week: Wednesday.
"Woe to you, Scribes and Pharisees."
St. Matt. xxiii. 1—36.

In a discourse addressed to the multitude and to His disciples, our Lord enjoins obedience to the Scribes and Pharisees as official exponents of the Law of Moses, but warns His hearers against imitating their works, and denounces them for their hypocrisy, formality, inconsistency, ambition, pride.

1. "Woe to you, Scribes and Pharisees!" This is a terrible denunciation coming from the mouth of God Incarnate. Christ thus denounces the Scribes and Pharisees because of (*a*) their self-exaltation. They love the first places at feasts, to be saluted as Rabbi, and to be accounted great. (*b*) Their hypocrisy. They make long prayers and profess great zeal, and meanwhile are guilty of scandal and injustice. (*c*) Their neglect of the essentials of the Law, judgment, justice, and truth, while they insist on the accidental duties of an exact payment of tithes and alms. (*d*) Their pretended indignation against the wickedness of their fathers in persecuting the prophets, while they themselves are just as bad. Examine yourself on these points, lest Christ say "Woe" to you.

2. All this corruption on the part of the Pharisees arose from their being puffed up by the respect shown to them by the people, and taking to themselves the honour paid to their office. This is a serious danger to all whose position entitles them to respect. They forget that those who occupy high places are bound for that very reason to esteem themselves the least and lowest.

3. How did the Scribes and Pharisees take our Lord's warnings? They were only the more embittered against Him. Woe to me, if I take reproof as they did.

Twenty-sixth Week: Thursday.
The Parable of the Ten Virgins.
St. Matt. xxv. 1--13.

There were ten virgins who went out to meet the bridegroom and the bride. Five were wise and five were foolish. The wise virgins took a good supply of oil in their lamps, but the foolish virgins took no oil. When the bridegroom came, the wise virgins were ready to meet him with lamps trimmed and burning. The foolish virgins, finding that their lamps had gone out, went to buy some oil and so were too late for the marriage, and were shut out.

1. The oil in the lamps of the virgins is the pure intention that makes us labour for God's glory, not for our own, and guide our lives by His holy inspirations and according to the Divine law, not by our own impulses and inclinations. Without this, the light that is in us is nothing else but darkness. Do I in my lamp carry this oil of Divine charity?

2. All ten were virgins, notes St. Gregory, but only five were admitted to the marriage-supper of the Lamb. It is not enough to be free from gross sin and do no harm. Without supernatural charity our natural virtues may even be a misfortune to us, if we trust to them and forget that they are worthless in the sight of God as a source of merit on earth or of glory in Heaven.

3. Those who were once shut out from the bridal feast vainly sought for admittance. Those who are shut out by the Particular Judgment from the Kingdom of Heaven are shut out for ever. What a terrible thought for me! How carefully I must watch, with the lamp of charity burning brightly. "Blessed is the man whom his Lord, when He cometh, shall find watching!"

Twenty-sixth Week: Friday.
The Parable of the Talents.
St. Matt. xxv. 14—30.

A man going into a far country gives to his various servants goods according to their ability. On his return the one servant who had received five talents, brought another five. Another, who had received two, brought another two, and so on. These servants are praised and richly rewarded by their master. One, however, who had received only one talent, had hidden it in the earth instead of trading with it. The master orders that he shall be cast into exterior darkness, and his talent given to the one who already has ten.

1. Observe that of those servants who have received much from God, far more is expected than from others. God has given me so much, so many opportunities for serving Him, so many endowments in the order of nature as well as graces beyond the average of men. God will expect of me a corresponding return.

2. The servant who had the smallest amount, was condemned for not employing it. If I have small talents, this will not excuse me if I neglect to use for God what I have. Notice, too, that this servant did not waste the money. His condemnation was for not gaining more for his master. It is not enough to do no harm. This will not save us; we must do positive good, if we wish to go to Heaven.

3. The graces that are neglected by some pass on to others. The talent of the idle servant is given to him that has gained the most by trading. How easy to lose graces! I must beware lest the graces God would fain have given me be bestowed elsewhere because of my ingratitude.

Twenty-sixth Week: Saturday.
The Final Judgment.
St. Matt. xxv. 31—46.

When the Son of Man shall come in His majesty, He will summon all mankind before Him; the just on His right hand, the wicked on His left. To the former He will say: "Come, ye blessed of My Father, inherit the Kingdom prepared for you from the foundation of the world." To the latter: "Depart, ye cursed."

1. Try to realize that day, when the whole world will be assembled, and you amongst them, before the throne of the majesty of Jesus Christ. On which side should you be found now? How will you endure to have all your hidden actions and secret thoughts made known to all? Have you not cause to tremble at that inevitable scene in which, whether you are willing or not, you must take a part?

2. The chief cause of terror to the wicked will be the wrath of Him who sits upon the throne as their Judge. His Divine beauty will make them long after Him, but His anger will make them long, in an agony of fear, to hide themselves from His sight. There is no misery to be compared to the misery of having Christ angry with us. Pray that you may never give Him cause to be angry with you.

3. The distinguishing mark between the just and the wicked is charity to others for Christ's sake. Christ speaks of this as the passport to Heaven. Not a word about any virtues save this. Why is this? Because self-denying charity for Christ's sake carries with it all other virtues and hides a multitude of sins. Is self-denying charity the distinguishing mark of my life?

www.ingramcontent.com/pod-product-compliance
Lightning Source LLC
Chambersburg PA
CBHW020845160426
43192CB00007B/787